THE SPIRAL SOUL OF HUMILITY & FORTITUDE

Chronicle 33

Panagiota Makaronis

KREA PREA (TM) Est. 2012

ISBN: 978-1-7644581-6-0

Cover design by:AI B3STOW
Editor: KREA PREA (TM) Est. 2012
Written: Craigieburn, Melbourne Victoria Australia

I Dedicate Chronicle 33 The Spiral Soul of Humility & Fortitude

To Melanie Makaronis

The Spiral of Life comes in many forms, we need structure, connection and Lineage. A balance to survive, Tests need to be created, lessons are to be learnt.

Troubles occur for several reasons, some need to learn lessons, Targeting the easy so they can get away with the damage they caused.

I call them addicts; substance abusers they like to enter your realm unwelcome. Those who have nothing better to do, go after he who harmed them right through.

Poisoning your spirit. People tend to attend to you at their worst, where it creates a common curse.
Giving you the indication you wish you never met them.

The foundation is the core essence and once that cracks your whole world turns upside down hitting you profusely. All while you're trying to get back on track.

Eventually the Storm after the fact will pass. You just need to be patient. There is no limitation, leaving a mark at your peak is part of Human Nature. A constant reminder that the certainty you carry within, will bring forth a united front.

A siren, then silence after the fact. To create a divine purpose, and keep humanity from losing its full Lustre.
I say release those demons that carry you, and attempt to poison your soul; just for one measly role.

Whether it's a family member or an acquaintance that will pick you up, or perhaps drag you down; you're just passing through. If the chase was made for you, time will tell; holding a grudge is Hell.

Whenever the trace has me face another brick wall. I found myself in that storm, Debris in every form. Where I have to break free, from that abreaction and remind myself I must, bring forth Humility Fortitude and comfort.

Because yesterday was the mark, today is a blessing. You never know what tomorrow will bring. For the journey you once knew, always brings forth solitude. Looking back and reminiscing is a step forward.

It brought you back to where it began, and broadened your Horizons. Where every step you took was just a gamble to help you Press replay.

Amen

PANAGIOTA MAKARONIS

CONTENTS

INTRODUCTION

The Spiral Soul of Humility and Fortitude; Chronicle 33, a method built on a Key, no longer surrendering or reminiscing. Because I hit the end of one chapter and the beginning of another. My freedom cut short, handing the corrupt a chance to repel, rebel and put me through hell.

A karmic effect that was part of a conspiracy, had me face an encore. Where that snake in the grass was humidified, no longer dehumanising my existence.

The underlying and undeniable truth, had come to be. That is when I knew, I hit a final degree. So, when I reached my peak, I could take a leap of faith, feed off the concept and break the chain. It had me reach my pinnacle and start again. A rude awakening to state a fact, and challenge that feast.

Forced off the edge, hounding me at every pledge. Questioning the motive and morals of those who lacked ethics and principals. It led me to embrace it all. Trapping those who return for one more flaw. A chance to reveal that upcoming beat. An assumption, that had served me a redemption.

A war was created in peace just to give that demon a chance to release. Those who were using me to claim their existence periodically had grounded me. My everlasting breath taken, on a journey that shocked the system. It had come to my reality after the fact; no chance in hell of repeating that tact.

I was left to debate what trace will hand me the case. It handed me a treasure to measure the truth. A final freedom to catch up, faced the corrupt with an entrance. It presented me with a clue; long overdue. Where they thought they had the energy to repeat rebel; against all odds. A forthcoming clue, a formality and a final reminder to skip that too, to get through.

It had me wondering, was I working with a veil of secrecy. Just to hand the corrupt a chance to return and belt me in advance. It forced me to repeat rebel and break that trend that put me through hell. It had me face a dead end. I was on trial prepared for one thing and that was to give in and face a new beginning.

The corrupt had a chance to meet me half way. They decided to push me off the edge, for they thought they had humility and strength to fight my spirit, and change me. They took me in then, broke the silence. Removing that veil of secrecy, a broken system from within; no freedom to win.

It prepared me for the last laugh, a warning that served me well. A thought pattern that was presenting with an upcoming spell. It gave me a chance to sweeten the deal, facing me with a brand-new case. A challenge that had me face a trace at the end of the race forcing me to undo a review.

I had to face a warning, a challenge that had me forced to hit back with a callback. I was put on a journey waiting for the right moment to repeat repel and face a window to an opportunity that had been pending. I was taken for a fool, left it to the imagination; causing no more defects.

As if I was chosen to put up with the corrupts poison, where I had to put up my guard. It left me fighting a lost cause, it took me on a journey that had me face chase and release peace. A chance to repeat, follow up on a treat. It forced me a journey that took me further than ever.

I was taken for a ride, torn in more than one direction. Just to give in and subdivide an inning. A challenge that was to serve me well, ended in failing a trace. It was handing me a forthcoming deserved desired hunt down. Returning for a favour at every meltdown.

Assuming I had a faith less likely to release that beast. For that beast served me a feast, it handed me a foundation that broke me at every manifestation. I was taught a lesson trapped in the middle, trying to catch up and face another trace. A turning event, where the spell took over the event.

I was left to recreate a trend that served me well in the end. The curse I was given had me face another revision. I was torn in more than one direction, taught a lesson and left it to chance, trapped in the middle of a ritual that was handing the corrupt a chaos in advance.

I was to delve into a trance stir the pot while I give in and face a win. The difference was the trace was based on a case that handed me a clue. It gave me a second chance to review a turn of events. It was handing me the outcome to that sitcom, longing to cancel that rerun.

An urge to return, fight back and face a trip down memory lane, had me survive another dive. A service provided, handed me a forthcoming spell. A trial towards a trace that had me piece together a final vendetta. Search for Peace, a knowing within my heart; I became a true victim to scrutiny.

I returned to prove my theory, only to sense I was working with the devil's presence. A challenge that come my way, was the last thing that had me forced to press replay. What I went through was unprecedented. It took me on journey that chased me towards the unknown.

Where the corrupt assumed, if I fell for the lie, it will break my spirit. Far from the truth, my purpose was stronger than the lie, the trace became part of a given to hand me a proposal. I needed to disembark on a path and engage with the corrupt. Enter that realm and rebel against their will.

I entered a disheartening challenge, a remorseful environment that took me down. It caused an effect and handed me a threat a need to pay off a debt. For the allegation was a test, forced me to repeat a feat. So, when I reached my pinnacle, I could press delete leaving the corrupt praising me.

That process was forming an alliance. It was leaving forced to hit back with remorse. I was handed a trial that served the corrupt a chance to push me off the edge. Waiting for me to pledge, trying my luck to fight back and feed off the impact. There was no trace, the trend was based on a past case.

The end result was a given, a chance to return for one

more season. I fell straight into a trance, trying to come to terms with the fact that the investigation led me towards a final validation. It presented me with a clue, handing me the second coming. It had the corrupt, returning for a yearning.

Stirring the pot, trying to claim another informative vision. A game that had me gamble everything away. My luck changed the corrupt returned to hand me an omen. Where the energy I needed to shake that tradition, had me depleted. Because they cheated there was no acceptance to that lead.

It created a deterrent effect, that handed me a threat. It had them come after me with utter regret trying to suppress my energy so I lose my cause, all while they continue to pause. The one that held me up, kept me hostage and left me to repeat and follow up on a trace; I could not erase.

It had me on the edge applauding the corrupts method; torn trying to get through. All so I pledge leaving me suffering in silence, hoping in hindsight it all ends well. Forgiven not forgotten, with no added regret. It was all an exaggeration to hand the corrupt a dead end, to that manifestation.

It was a test to make me bleed. All so I can repeat start again, create an invasive intrusion, to those who used me and handed me confusion. A trace to repeat another test, a given conquest to hand me a faith less likely to eradicate. I was brave, I took a challenge, and fell into a trap; gunning it.

Led towards an awkward event, a destination; enforced the obvious. I was to award those who were sitting on my raider assuming I was their meal ticket to the next stage. There was no limit only an obligation and a constant reminder I was hitting a scam. A redemption an overall failed resurrection.

It had me face a repetition to my mission, thrown into the deep end. Feeding off that scenery breaking the eve. Handing me the invasion to break the cycle. I had to face a vision preparing me for one more competition. I was at breaking point, between the old new and the fire that broke through.

I hit the end of an awakening, from that trend. It served me the will to break free from that skill. For the corrupt used me as an easy target, waiting for me to return for another feast. What a test I had to release just to find peace from justice of the Peace. The journey they put me on was pointless.

Out of sight out of mind, just to hand justice, to those who overrode the system. Caused effects use me as their muse, corner me with no freedom to amuse me; just abuse me so they never loose. Left feeling exhausted, defeated no fortitude to release that beast. Forced to remain silent and resilient.

A villain to a game created a piece. Remained vigilant to a certain key, where my name had me unreasonably intact. Trying my luck to hit me simultaneously, delete delay and follow up on another damn replay. Just to give the Gluttony a chance to build a portfolio; bribing me every step of the way.

They had me sitting in the Loop, strong minded holding on to a dream that was long gone. Before I had a chance to line up for another conspiracy. It was part of a damn threat, that was meant to lead me towards a direction of rejection detection and a lifelong debt; that was not considered bright.

Wasting time and valuable energy feeding off the trace that had me face another given, case. Where everything that come to be had me facing another fake reality. They had me trapped creating a piece that will bring forth solitude to their safety net. All while I was faced my truth to that reality.

I felt threatened to the core, the only thing that served me well from within was the challenge. A task had me withstand the truth. Trying to catch up, break the chain face a case while I remain brave while I start again. Treating me as an entitlement instead of an independent.

It was feeding off my inner core, an essence of my dismemberment. An awakening where my inner voice became an enigma to that stigma. It served me well, handed me a trace that put me through hell. What a journey I had to unveil, just to teach the corrupt a valuable lesson.

The manipulation and the gaslighting once again became part of a given trend. I had to chase away a demon who was sitting patiently in my peripheral vision. All while I gave in and broke the system, the foundation that made me easy. Because they were put in a position worse than the imagination.

Interrogating me, at every follow up became an extremity that handed me anxiety. I found myself hiding in the corner, I could not understand why I was blamed while the others were instigating a fight. The momentum changed and so did my views, I was disregard completely.

Time will tell, and eventually take over the game, where the turn for worst will get better. Because the rumour that caught up blew up like a time Bomb. Where the trend will eventually die down in the end. The inner soul creates a trace; it haunts you with no means to an end.

Over all, if you do not serve your purpose and you ignore the signs; limitations are endless. It puts you through hell. The ambition becomes an entrance, trying to reverse a curse. Serve those who used you to declare, there freedom. A pathway, leading you towards insanity instead creditability.

Breaking the cycle that leaves you hunting for good will instead of serving it.

AMEN

CHAPTER 1

◆ ◆ ◆

A Journey Through The Fire No Flame In Sight

What an offer I was handed, when corrupt had me branded, facing another enigma. Not only did they return for a yearning, but I could not help thinking I was a victim to the system. He who knew planted a seed and left me brewing over it so when the time come, I fail and they succeed.

They had me locked in, creating a war in my peace. Where the only way out was I looking to follow up on a past remorse. No regret just a venture that will lead the corrupt towards a brand-new sector. I was to hand them failure, constant doubt. An opportunity to confess, and face that test.

The dream turned into a drama in-between, face a true royal flush. Where I ended up blue and the corrupt ended up green with envy. Where they took me in and faced me with a true-blue reality check. Making me out to be a fool, leading me to a destination; no worse than the resection.

Where the energy that created the piece forced me off the edge. I was made out to be the stalker the perpetrator while the rest were catching up watching my progress feeding off my success. Seemingly fans of my work, could not wait to steal my identity, paying attention to every detail.

It faced me with a trace, turned my light dim and handed the corrupt a second chance to get in and win everything. This time around entering my realm was no longer common ground. It was the wrong path, though they had the energy to get in and intimidate; the end result ended in tragedy.

A journey that will harm them in mind body and soul. A whimsical effect that sold me out with a whirl wind effect. I was handed fascistic role, concocting of ways to break me so I never succeed. Instead of handing them validation, I held my head up high fell in a lie and continued on my journey.

All so the corrupt don't enter and face me with a tremor. The given proof was a condition to sweeten the deal and hand me a competition. Where they take that as permission to slay towards another direction. So, they never enter my realm unwelcome. I cut them off I wished them harm.

I had no choice I had to rejoice, for the road I was on had me hit a dead-end outcome. Made sure they knew when I reached my pinnacle; they never get through. For every competition will serve them a failed proposition. A journey that had nothing offer but a failed test to that conquest.

I was way more profound let's say, I Caused an Effect and fell into hell, trying to claim catch up and not lose my way. I was so caught up in those webs of lies. An interaction to that deception that had me facing another abreaction The more they fought back the less I will portray.

The less they saw the better, but I had nothing to give, I was stuck trying to live. Hiding my light was too hard, to release. I had no time to fight back the drama took over and instilled while it shifted and turned black. because I was shining way to bright. The shimmer took the corrupt by surprise.

It gave them a chance to have me wither, all while I suffer and they win. The trace became a new beginning, a challenge that left me whinging and denying me access. It served a warning that created a yearning that forced me off the straight and narrow. I fell into a ditch pledging what I knew.

Creating a brand-new review, stirred the corrupts plot. They had me stand my ground stepping into the unknown forcing me to return to face a given, before I hit the forbidden. I fell, had to heal from the wound, fight anxiety while I follow it up. A treat, trapped in the middle of that good deed.

All while they were trying to feed off me simultaneously. So, when I reached my pinnacle, I would hit back with a faith less likely for me to get back on track. What a test I had to fortress, just to cave in on the final contest a concept from within had me face another whimsical concept.

Yearning for a return before the corrupt could entrap had me face a given. A proposition that served me the loyalty card. Where I needed to remain lined up for a given train of thought. A trend that had me forced to repeat had me remain idling all while the rest enter my realm unwilling to serve me.

Unravelling Gods will, was not part of the entry; it handed me the wrong intention. It had me facing a brand-new revelation. The motive was unprevented it had to run its course unprecedented. The action that was given handed me a final abreaction. lined up for a dead end a mission resolved.

The trace became forced and I had to remain idling to the game. It had me hit a hard truth and that was the corrupt had no intention of helping me move forward. I had to come to terms with the fact I was on my own here wasting no time. I made my mark reached my pinnacle mastered my craft.

I had to endeavour to devour every final tremor. Just to claim remain sane break the chain reaction that served me a final abreaction. I hit a dead end, but my creativity kept intact, it kept me on the road building my luck, trying my best to face that resilience. A momentum that held me to ransom.

A sense of being was handing me the loyalty, a trend forcing me to repeat repel and start again. The corrupt stalled, long enough for me to reveal and follow up on another given a restoration. I had to face a rejection, to that manifestation that had reached its peak and handed me a rude awakening.

Where this time around it had me sitting in reception waiting for Admin to hand me validation. A conspiracy that took over my journey and forced me to reveal what truly happened. I was taken for granted and the corrupt had me facing a raw deal a challenge that weighed me down.

It left me hunting for common ground, I was to feed off that final entrance, to the unknown. A warning that served me the willingness to hit back with earnest. A challenge that served me the ease to hit a practicality from that cease. When I reached my pinnacle, could undo follow up on a review.

It had me forced to hit back and break the silence from within. Just to help me get back what was owed and who used me to get through. They were handing me a loss from that redemption a trial an error and final a faith, less likely for me to feel terror. Part of a trace that had me forced to give in.

I was left to praise those who were part of the problem. One false move, on my end and they will return, handing me more complications. It made them look extremely inviting, I wanted them out of my life. Leave me to live in peace, they saw me as a threat, could not wait to return belt me again.

They were envisioned by my vision; my presence was handing them entertainment. I felt I was unleashing an unwanted effect. I entered a realm that served me well it forced me to give in face another warning. While I was attempting to get in and win another inning, I become traumatised.

I felt the prize slip through my fingers; I was led on left to relive a nightmare so the corrupt can remain strong. I was torn in more than one direction hitting a faith less likely for me to reach that final resurrection. I was running the risk of being forced to reminisce a final case to that trace.

I had to unleash before I hit an encore, a step forward towards a final degree. Handing the corrupt their last chance to belt me in advance a new review to hit back with an overview. It was part of an overcast that handed me my first and last overlapping that everlasting clue.

A chance to see I had no freedom nor foundation to return for a hailed event. For what I knew to what was meant to be true, became a motive that handed the corrupt their last return. For I hit the end of that trauma that had me face another drama. I had to fast forward to the next destination.

Haunted by the past, living in the present warned to run hide and not face a self-destruction from that overdrive. A forthcoming event had come and gone over written leading me towards becoming bedridden. I felt uneased absolutely turned, up and down trying to get out of that domination.

It was holding me to ransom, as if I was being targeted by a true inhumane demon. Appealing to those who were unfaithful, it had me stepping into disloyalty for that trauma sent me further. I could not remind myself anymore, what had come from that outcome all I knew I hit a first and last clue.

The retrace to that case had me face a warning. It caused an effect had me pay out a debt so when I reached my pinnacle, I was back where I started and this time, I hit a final. Waiting for the corrupt to serve me an unwilling denial. I was left behind serving the wrong, hitting a final encore.

I should have let it go, but it was hard I had a lot riding on it. The journey I chose was not morose but those who knew, where I was heading were humbly on my raider once again pushing me in the corner. All so I hit a beheading, a challenge that had me face my inner beauty.

In the end I gave in, I served myself, no freedom to return. My foundation hit an upturn. I had to please the inner me, before I fell into a dead-end. They took me in and forced me to run a mile and fail every trial. I had to face my true reality an inner force that had me freely return, for remorse.

In fact, it was part of a game that served me the same test. From a treat to a trap a task to help me overlap and get back what is owed. A trial to serve me well and hand me denial. It had me serving the corrupt within a turn that lined me up for a feast that heaved at me at the end of that piece.

I was not to look, back; but it was difficult to let it slide there was to prejudice I had lost my chance to hit back in advance because the trap had me surrender all inhabitations. There were several on my raider waiting to see when I fail so they can sail. They cheated the system and left me suffering.

I was silently, and repetitively living in denial, creating a piece. No warning, just a yearning to keep me from failing. It gave the corrupt a chance to release, and I second chance to return delete delay, forcing the corrupt to play it my way. It was a given, it had me praise the wrong, as I raise awareness.

The corrupt took an ingenuity and turned into a fight. It led me towards a journey that had me ripen my soul raise the buck and trap them. Where all I wanted to do was cut them out of my life. For they were intruding in my affairs, facing me with a flare that did not make it to the air.

I had hit a final interrogation from that manifestation. Only to witness the road I was on brought me towards an ending that taught me a lesson. An ingredient, that pushed the corrupt in the corner, off the edge, no room to state a fact nor even pledge. Served me well handed me a dirty trick too.

A forthcoming evaluation, to that manifestation, handed me the truth. It gave me a second chance to hit the corrupt in advance. Forcing them to redo replace and face another driven momentum to that road that handed me a clue. leading the corrupt to destination with no validation.

Where they no longer use one another to get through. With any luck they return, turn against one another right through. Hitting a dead end in the end and a hold up where their friendship hands them hardship. Repeating a new improved final clue so when I catch up, I can replace it all.

The old the new the upcoming clue force the corrupt to stand their ground and follow up on a given sustained event. The one choice needed for me to return and follow up on a clue and vent right through. All so I can claim what I thought was the everlasting trace, at the end of the race.

It also handed me the energy to set it all free, break that cycle that served me a challenge that hit me at arrival. The thought I had when I hit that road was wrong, I was not aware I was saving he who was watching me from afar. Leading me to a destination where I lose all concentration.

Where they took me in, with a debate a deliberate observation to face me with an instigation. I was heading for a fight trying my luck to get back on track and face another given. It was handing me the proposal I needed to reach my peak. I had to make sure the corrupt never return hit with the rough.

No ride to the other side, no challenge to silently survive. I was left in the middle trying to come to terms with the fact the journey was harsh. A rude awakening, the only way I could redo was replace the old the new and the forthcoming review. All while I fast forward to the next turn of events.

I had to repeat release that beast that had me enforced to hit back with remorse. All because the trace was a given a trend forbidden and every motivation ended in a dead-end investigation. A manifestation praised by those who created a trace that served me a willingness to erase.

I hit back with a sturdiness no further than imagined. No trace nor trap to cancel because the corrupt saw me as an easy target. forced to review so when the time come, I can serve them a final outcome. Lining me up for a dead end in the end, with a trick then a trip down memory lane

A prize given by the almighty. It served me a hard truth a challenge that caved in on the concept. It prepared me for a review that handed me a renewal. A concept that saw me fight back and feed off the energy that had me revolving into the next final case that handed me a dead-end in the end.

CHAPTER 2

◆◆◆

The Genetic Pool A System You Cannot Rule

The mission was done and I was the other side protecting myself from that outcome. For I found the corrupt were on a mission to make sure I don't make it to the next proposition. They were pretending keeping me occupied on their raider, so I lose trapped yet again foreclosing a dead end.

For that journey was never ending, they had me facing a violation that hit me with a final admiration. Projecting that trend, so I don't have to put up with another failed attempt. I was hit with a conspiracy in the end. I had to go back, open that gate and let them those bats out free.

Just to give the corrupt a final challenge a dead-end in the end. For they had me holding on to a trace that served me well at the end of the race. It had me face another trace it gave me a trial and error and a final dilemma that took me on a journey.

It served me a clue forcing me to follow up on anther review. For he who knew, wanted to face me with a curse that served me a trace that had me face an upcoming case. It forced me to repeat restore and breach another challenge at the end of the race. Preparing me for one more trace.

I was pushed to create a barrier, for the curse was to be reversed it had me face another bad omen waiting for the corrupt to return and hit me with failed attempt, to catch up and break that tradition that had me hit repetition A war in between the old the new and the creative review.

For the corrupts piece, had me face another trace forcing me to repeat that everlasting beat. I had to look within find peace preparing myself for another feast. A trace that served me a case it gave me a chance to delve into a journey that led me astray holding me hostage every step of the way.

A creative sense that serviced the corrupt well, it had me stand my ground waiting for he who knew to return and face me with another invasion to that manifestation. They prepared me for one more key, it forced me off the edge returning the favour and favouring me.

With one more tremor in mind, I had to read between

the lines ready to sail and prevent me with another trial error and constant reminder the journey was not part of the method. It was part of a conspiracy that served me a will save me in the long run. It had me forced to hit back with remorse.

It saw me easy blocking another feast, a space in between here there and everywhere. There I was again hitting a challenge waiting for the trace to encourage me to erase. That is when I knew I hit a dilemma a task that restored my energy, facing me with a reification at the end of that destination.

I was given a chance to repeat, a challenge, that served a cleanse there was drama in the middle with a trace that had me face another case in the end. It had me reap a reward at every mission. Forced to hit a second trial, a trend that served me a revival. Hit back with cover up on my back.

For several who knew, took me in and face me with a tremor that served me a dilemma from within. They were causing effects, trapped me in the middle and forced me to enter that realm untouched. I had to embrace what I thought was part of an everlasting key. A challenge that served its purpose.

Forced off the edge straight into a delayed conquest. A dilemma that broke me when I fell into a trivial effect. It had me enter that realm unprecedented, so when it ended, I could come out looking excellent. For that trend will remain solvent, and the last thing standing continue to strengthen.

It had me hunting for my rights facing another dilemma. For that whole conspiracy was a joke it had me facing another warning, where the corrupt were feeding me handing me my rights. It caused an effect pushed me off track created a given and presentation that had me entering damnation.

With a failed attempt that had me convey and uncover up another bad day. It got me in and served me a willingness to claim another game, force my way in trap the corrupt from within. I had start again warning me I had no freedom nor foundation to break the cycle and the system.

I hit a median, a cussing effect where everything went wild. My whole world collapsed serving the wrong and preparing for a heat of the moment a challenge that had me forced to hit back with a reminder I was way off track. It had me hitting a defect at the end of that trend.

Served a challenge that had me coverup another trend. I wanted to get in and get another crack at it. But all it did had me regain a conscious awareness. I was hit with deception face another redemption, created a solvent that lined me up for a dead end. An effect that bribed me in the end.

It was pushing me off the edge, so I fail creating a back lash of denial. I was not aware I had several on my raider stepping into my dome. Hoping I would fail and end up six feet under before my time. I was leading the pack feeding off the concept waiting for the corrupt to hit me with a challenge.

It led me towards a journey that forced me off the edge, straight into a dilemma that had me fail, I hit a silent reaction to that manifestation. It had been troubling my head for so long the corrupt were on my raider trying to come up with ways to astound me with method to lead me astray.

All while they were trying to get ahead, leaving me humble facing another wrong move waiting for me to fail so they can continue to sail. I had to repel and follow up on another spell; a trace given where I had to face another trial error and another final upkeep from that vendetta.

A scheme that forced me to redeem faced another trace. For I was warned at the end of that common race. For the mission had the corrupt concocted with a final deception. It was part of a competition that served me an overzealous path. Where every journey I was on saw red.

That is when I knew I was never going to get through. To many beltings not enough support, in the end I gave in I could not fight back. There were to many ganging up on me leaving me suffering in silence while they resurrect. The rest sail through helping themselves while feeding off the rumour.

I was a fool to think that those who knew were praising me. It was a curse I could not reverse for everything was rehearsed. For those who knew were facing a review. It had me trapped in the middle of a wrap, a constant reminder there was no key. My faith was taken by chance to rebel.

I had to repeat and face another upcoming spell. A challenge that took me in and forced me to repeat repair and escape another challenge so I can claim and envision the game independently. It was forcing me to revive a dive and face that given. hitting me with a curse adding to my scars.

It had me forced to hit back with remorse. Where I became the problem instead of the solution, they got their wish used me to get there and when the time come use me again. Where this time around I was led to believe the drama was deprived and every momentum had me face another dive.

The enemy became part of a trend, that taught me a valuable lesson in the end. There was no energy to succumb, just a final outcome. For that solidarity that had me face another outcome had me forced to hit an ending that was causing the wrong effects.

Repugnant as it was, I still had to show up and put up. Pray to God that the energy that served me then took over that trace that had me face another given. A red-hot vision that lined me up for one more competition. It took me on a journey that served me a priority; first and last.

A key to save me at my best had me face another request. For last thing that was written was a given reason to hit back and face me with another treason.

It led me astray laughed at, all the way. That is when I knew I hit abroad and the only thing that had me face an interest was cause an effect.

I had to face a turn of events, that had me on the edge. An ending to that trend that forced me to look back not forward in the end. All because I fell into a trap, that took me on a journey back on track. I went through it all, a drama, added with an error, then have me go back to where it began.

Here I was again the old the new and the end of what I thought will bring me forward. In fact, I was forced to hit back with remorse and repeat another tremor so I can claim and hit back with a vibe that served me well and kept me alive. I entered the unknown unworthy, and unwelcome.

Everyone who knew back then had me repeat and start again. Instead of the corrupt helping me get through they found opportunity to come after me. Then blame me for every final review, crafty as they had forced me off the edge, so I never pledge or return for one more given reason thread

It had me facing a traumatic event I could not see the positive side all I saw was the corrupt ready and willing to hit me with Genocide. Where I could see I had no strength to fight back for I was way to cut up and the corrupt were to erupt. I could not reclaim or even sustain a vision to the game.

It was as if they had me in locked in inbound ready to face me and feed off me from within. With no freedom to win. For they were really friendly, fake false and misleading and instead of facing me with an entrance they took me in and fed off me from the beginning.

That is when I knew they had me ready and willing to give in, God Willing. I was on the road to nomad's land. Several years of Bad Luck had passed and every seven years became a blast. An extra three had developed to give the corrupt a chance to return and read all about it.

Assuming what I write will be used against me. But what I write are stories fables I don't mean to harm. Nor do I want to burn, it tore me apart everyone I met wanted to see me depart from this world sooner than later. It caused a lot of conflict; for everyone I met then hate me now.

Everyone I meet now, judge and hate me no benefit of the doubt. All because those who I met back when purely played it, so I never say it or start again. I'm in the position right now that makes me wonder what the point is, why bother. Only to witness the drama was not mine it was all a lie.

It was nice for those who hit ran and decided what my destiny would be like. All so I fail give in and lose my identity from within, just to catch a break and pray to God that every feast served me a piece just to sweeten the deal and follow up on a tremor to hand me a false reading.

A final meeting, that had me reprieve served me a sentence and failed me in between. All because those who need me are bloody greedy and needy. Assuming the worst of me will hand them a curse. Return the favour threefold trying to repeat reclaim and press delete hitting me with a wonder.

Even when the trace had me forced to replace, I was still stuck trying my luck ready and willing to face another revelation to that destination. It had me face a trace create a piece forced me to foreclose another feast at the end of that piece. It had me return the favour and press replay.

Pending to lead the way, had me surrendering my truth to claim another bad day. All because I wrote a few stories, and those stories opened up Pandoras box. A huge can of worms giving the corrupt a chance to return for a rerun, belt me in advance. Leaving me struggling to claim my truth.

I'm here to feed their greed and hand them a second chance to succeed. For what reason only those who knew forced me to hit back and have me face another review. For what reason only the energy that served me a free rode had me face and prepare for a hell forsaken ride.

What is wrong with society today where do I begin where do I end it all. Where those who fed off me to get to where they are; are fighting me now. All because I refuse to allow them to continuously to latch on and feed off my energy to remain strong. But all it did was force me to fight back.

It had me face another Law of attraction, instead of

rising above it all. I fell into a trap that left me fighting back. All for a key, that was stollen from me. Now that I am here and made it to the end of that passageway; fighting that demon that served me a reason to hit back with treason.

Trying to retrieve a damn good deed. For what good it did, I could not state, for I was given a reason to repeat and repel against that truth that served me a well earnest look from within. Waiting for me to catch up and face another trace. Releasing a demon that forced me into an oblivion.

I was still stuck trying to get out of that rut. But all it did was warn me I was in the deep doing it hard. Making things worse and trying to come to terms with the curse. I had no freedom to fight back and the corrupt were blessing me with a curse I had to reverse, researching ways to push me off track.

I gave in, because it was part of a yearning, for all I wanted was to rewrite my piece in peace. But I had come to terms with the fact I hit Justice of the Peace. A challenge that had me meet and greet and follow up on another preach trapped in the middle of a long-lasting effect.

A trace where every gamble forced me to release the beast at the end. I was left to pretends given a reason to leave it to treason. So, when I reached my peak, the only thing holding me hostage weas the last thing that had me face another trace at the end of that win.

They threat became a debt and I had no freedom to repent. I had to release that beast that had me forced to hit back with remorse. I was praised with a pointless affair; an absolute doubt had come crashing down. Warning me there was no foundation or freedom to reclaim another competition.

I was made out to be the perpetrator, a liar the cheat all of the above just to meet the corrupts criteria. Nothing said was true. I was a victim of scrutiny giving he who knew a second chance to get a crack at harming me too. Where in true fact I hit a bad omen forced to hit back with a warning.

A learning curve became part of a challenge that had me immerse into a past curse. Where the given momentum handed me on the edge wrapped up ready to pledge. While all along I had been given a trace it handed me a clue and forced me to review. All while I took it all in and fell into a warning.

For the time had come and I needed to replace the old the new and forthcoming clue. I was rebelling against those who were trying their luck to hand me bad luck. I had to report and follow upon another trend in the end. Trapping me while I got caught up in a lie to get by.

Where I was given a chance to repeat and report, take it all in and face another win. A follow up on a trace that had me face another curse. The one that was ready and willing to be reversed. In the end of that trend the journey I once knew became part of a dead-end.

Where every journey passed, it caused an effect, as if a seed was planted. I was to return and be branded a task that gave the corrupt a chance to belt me in advance. It presented me with a brand-new huge debt. Where I needed to return budget and start again just to find peace from within.

For that means to an end, had me facing a journey that had me repeat. I had to report and follow up another fort. I was taught a lesson and left it to chance, all because the corrupt saw me as a victim to a plot they concocted working on it for years it got to the point I was left to irate another trait.

All so I never rise above and beyond m giving into every forthcoming song. For that trial was served and that trace reserved. There were several were on my raider planting seeds trying to decide of what my destiny should be in-between. Here I was again on my own lining up for another truce.

A hold up towards a fold up had me face a trace where I gave in. Grieved at every challenge from within. Handing me a fight that took me on a journey that served me wrong. Where it was meant to serve me right all along. In the end I became a recluse, just to find peace from that broken fuse.

A trace that had me repeat a case, had me replace a trace, then without warning retrieve a follow up I hit another good deed, handed a review a follow on another clue. So, when I caught the corrupt in the middle of a riddle the challenges that served me were well adjusted.

I was forced towards a journey that served me a warning. It handed me a key to sweeten the deal and feed off the journey that had me forced to hit back with remorse. I had to help the corrupt get back on track. There was several working under the raider warning others to play it too.

CHAPTER 3

◆ ◆ ◆

Releasing The Demon That Sweetened The Deal

It got to the point my freedom to walk out the door was cut short. I had no foundation to renew and no preparation to repeat that destination that had me locked in. They were waiting for me to sail while the rest prevail. Lining me up for a competition that had manifested.

There was no validation, just a whole lot of lies that became part of the corrupts final uproar. A deceit that served me a final feat, and a challenge that helped me delete delay and press replay. So, when I reached the end of that trend, the outcome served me well and presented me with a key.

Where every entrance had me locked in. None of them had purpose all were sorrowful preparing for dead ends in the end. Trying to reclaim a driven from that admission, handing me a competition. It was part of a follow up of a past deceit where I found myself hitting an ending that was pending.

A trace that was unbelievable, took its toll, it just did not make any sense in the end. I was led on left to suffer so the corrupt can remain strong. It had me remain silent while the rest forced me to undo following up on a clue. Every quest had me foreclose another find; a trace that messed up my head.

The end of the race became part of a tremor it had me return and feed of the endeavour. A follow up where the curse had me undo break every chain reaction from within. I was hit in between the lying the cheating and the underlying thing that had me face another inning.

Weighed down from that final train of thought. Where the only thing that warned me from within was the way in and even then, I had to fight another trace that had me replace the old the new and the upcoming review. It had forced me to press replay, every step of the way.

I was to give in and feed off the outcome that was unravelling a trace from within. I became the vampire to the Victim, that was pretending that I was the perpetrator trying to cover up another force to hit me with remorse. All while I was given a reason to endure another treason.

I had to lie then try my luck to embrace a trace. It served

the corrupt a challenge, handing me the end result that forced me to reclaim that precious proposal. It served me a vision creating a war in between here there and everywhere. Where I envisioned a better angle at the end of the game.

Not only I was let down, but I caved in on the concept too and found myself in a position worse than the mission. it was a challenge that turned many heads and many bystanders against me. That is when I knew I hit the end of that trend forced to renew and face another review.

I had nowhere to go, nowhere to turn for help everyone who was on it created a war in my piece. Because I kept to myself, there lie became half the truth. The other half had been pending leading me to a destination that served me the wrong end of the trend facing me with a dead end.

It forced me to release facing another feast, handing me a rebate, just to find peace. Leading me to a destination that had me face a rebellious investigation. For what it was worth it forced me to rely on nobody to get by because those who knew wanted to face me a follow up on another review.

It had me reach my peak and follow up on anther given. Just so I can catch up and claim the written report from the forbidden case a challenge that served me a warning and hit me with a yearning. A clever response that served me a review and forced me to hit back with an upcoming expense.

A faith less likely to release had me forced to undo a clue. Harmed spiritually right through. The beast, from that feast was hunting me down and haunting me from one entrance to the next. There I was again forced to sit back and wait for the corrupt to return and fight back.

That is when I knew I hit a final. No one was coming back; I was now reliving a nightmare. They hit me, laughed about it too I could sense my reality turn into true trial an error, a final vendetta. They got me down and left me feeling as if everyone I met were against me.

The troubled that followed served me my eulogy. I gave in, I could not fight back I had no freedom nor the fellowship what I had was a final championship. It felt those who I knew were following them too. A trait that weighed me down and left me forced to hit back with an upcoming verse.

I was on my own lined up for a new crown, my goals and my achievements were ignored. because those who were in on it, were aiming and goal setting to. Trapping me in their world hoping I will return so they can force me in the corner and face me with a wrongdoing.

In the end I felt as if belting me will serve them well. I felt uneased left to hit an ending and a constant reminder the journey was purely for me to suffer. Handing them an upcoming stream of events that led me towards a journey that forced me to vent.

Only to witness I hit a final degree a challenge that fussed over me way too much. A gift that kept giving and a task that was hard to respite. It forced me off the edge straight into a cause an effect. Warning me the only thing that come to be was the last thing that had me served.

In the end that trace was the beginning of a brand-new trend. This time, without doubt or a word of lie I was stuck trying to accept defeat and keep defiant; mocking those who were reliant. Try not allowing my pride to sustain and fail me at the end of that trend. Because in the end it was a game.

Gambling that final endeavour, forcing my way through. True to my word trapped in the middle a final riddle. A vendetta that took me in and faced me with a trial and an error from within. Where the corrupt got what they came for. They got me down and kept belting me.

Instead of me letting go I kept them there, waiting for the troubles to subside. It had me feed off the need, and claim another breed, so when I reached the end of that road the beginning was starting to look overlooked. I had no freedom to undo that clue that held me hostage right through.

I was taught a lesson by those who used me to get there. They caused an effect forced their way in even trapped me in the middle of an upcoming spin. I was entering an inning forced to hit back with a warning so when the time come, I could overcome another outcome to the system.

All so they never face a traditional case, I was lied to left to hit back with a trace that served me a trial an error and a final vendetta. I was facing another trend at the end of that chaotic event; it forced me to hit back with an expense that was creating a war in my peace.

Where the only thing that brought me forward was the last thing that had me face another trend from within. In the end of that chaotic event, there was a challenge that took me down. It lined me up for one more thing before I began to reserve another inning from within.

For that trace had me step into a cause, it had me repeat a trend at the end of that personal vision. I was trying my luck to hit back with a proposition. It caused an effect took me in faced me from within, lining me up for one more chance to return for one more yearning.

A warning that took its toll had me face one more vision from that competition. It had me face a warning hit back with a yearning, so when I caught up the only thing that was withstanding was the last thing that served me well from within. Troubled with a choice I could not make or reserve.

It served me well and forced me to reclaim another version to the game that had me forced to start again while I faced another presentation at the end of that game. It lined me up for one more key, a given reason to hit back with treason. A challenge that had me return for one more thorn.

All because the journey I was on had me face a trial and an error, with a final vendetta. It was part of a given, that had me challenge that test that served me well at the end of that conquest. For that truth warned me I was nowhere near I was meant to be. Served a willingness to hit back.

There was no final and the trace was a hint that had me face a trip down memory lane. It took me further than ever. I was allegedly confronted with a first and last curse, a given reason to repeat and reclaim another enforcement to a game that was troubling me all the same.

It had me on the edge trapped in the middle of a cover up. Where I was given a challenge worse than the energy that had me face another disgrace. I had to claim a cathedral of energy. Stepping into a program that had me face another trace. There was no given reason to hit back with treason.

Warning me there was no cause and effect, just a final reservation to hand me a clue. A clear trace that had me forced to repeat and replace. Where every warning served me a yearning, for what it was it handed had me a clue a face that turned everything against my free will.

A trace, that forced me to replace, gave me a second chance to return and hit back in advance. For what it was worth, it had me face another encore, to that final feast. For the journey was too hard to release I had to convey and that was enough for me to press replay.

For the trace was a given, to convince me to play it the corrupts way. It caved in on me and forced me to hit back with what I thought was last resort. Creating a challenge that will serve me well it gave me the power and the entertainment I needed to push me through hell.

It came to the point, the troubles that followed had me face a trap. A tradition from past competition that led me towards a journey that face d me at the end of that yearning that broke the system and fed off me at every informal proposition. For what it was worth the case was closed.

Those who used me to claim that lie, are about to face a journey. A follow up on another given, a chance to hit back with a curse. Just to help me revive, reverse and follow up on another given curse. For those who gave in, served their sentence and handed me the validation to win from within.

For that will to harm them in mind body soul made my spirit cringe. It served its purpose but at what price only those who knew could undo and follow up on another clue. For it turned in to a curse that served me the wisdom to follow up on another verse.

There was a trace that had me face another trend that served me a will to hit back with a brand-new skill. A challenge that took me in and forced me to revive another enigma to stay alive. For I was trapped in a dramatic effect, that had me forced to hit back with another debt.

The journey was harsh, the trace erased and the trend was too hard to compete compel and take a moment to embrace another forthcoming spell. Where the Demon from hell will create a demonic effect from within, where the corrupt will never get in and win another inning from within.

The will to return and have the corrupt feed off the cold hard truth, had me stand my ground. It gave me a second chance to hit back in advance. Where the end of that trend caused an effect, a will to embrace the truth. Hinting to me the task created a mask, that will return and feed off me whole.

It made wonder, what really happened and why did I fall in that mess. Was it to get the corrupt to confess, or was it to save myself from a hardcore truth. A contest that had me hit the end of my tither sitting pretty waiting for the corrupt to stir the pot. Hit with a force that served me remorse.

A debt that was outstanding, was a challenge that was withstanding. It had me face an event that forced me to repeat replace and face a forthcoming case. So, when the corrupt traced the given thought, it will undo and feed off the tradition that served me well right through.

For that moment that mark the spot, had marketed its truth. It had me face a trace at the end of the race. It had me refrain and face a trial, an error to a game that handed me a final vendetta. I was taken for a fool, left to repeat another rule. It took me in had me waste valuable time.

I was waiting to be heard taken for a ride, seriously no longer I was faced with a warning that had me forced to hit back with a reminder. For the corrupt had me on the edge trapped in the middle of a forthcoming riddle. Trying to catch up and face another trace at the end of that forthcoming curse.

It had me sense the only thing standing was the last thing I remembered before I hit end of that sacrament. It had me face another trace at the end of that trend. I was served and forced to hit back with an upcoming spell. Where the corrupt saw me as an easy target; feeding off my existence.

Heaving at me at every opposition making me feel less than. So, when the corrupt return they can continue to spread their venom and help me reform and start again. Feeding off the trauma that served me well in the end. For what it was worth the trace was a waste of a forthcoming case.

It warned me I hit an ending that was pending and a trace that was never going to come to fruition. Because the lack of tradition to the mission come to fruition. It was handing me the outcome I needed to get back on track and face another final impact.

It gave me a chance to validate, a final vendetta that lined me up for a warning. They were scheming at every trace redeeming that trial and error that served me a long line of hard ship. Leaving me forced to hit back with remorse. All while I violate a trace at the end of that forthcoming event.

For the journey was a given and every trace had me face a treason, for no apparent reason. Haunting me so I never see it all come to light. For those who had it in for me were on my raider trying to release another demonic feast.

Leaving me forced to return and hit back with one more key. A given reason to return and hit back for no reason, trapped in the middle of a forthcoming season. The riddle became a trial an error and a forthcoming adventure. They had me releasing that demon that saw me as an easy target.

Warning me there was no faith less likely to erase and no given reason to sweeten the deal and force me off the edge straight into a lead that had me return for one more good deed. It served me well creative trend that had me face a dead end at every disposal.

It took me on a journey, that led me towards a proposal; that had me solve every issue. Where I was left to repeat pledge, handing the corrupt a dead end at the end of that final trend. For every disposal created friction to that tuition handing me the cold hard truth.

I was led on left to remain strong, forced to hit back with a united front. So, when I reached the end of my tither, the trace became competitive, compelling and overrated. The conspiracy to hit me with a first and last cause, had me face the corrupt with a troubled head; ready to hit back with remorse.

They were on my raider forcing me to hit back, so I lose all perspective. For the corrupt had me chase a dream that was dramatic in-between. I was led on, left to repeat and follow up on another challenge. Hitting back with a vendetta that served me a role at the end of that tremor.

For they were trapped left to hit back and get back on track. Just so, they can return and get another crack at it. I was led on left to silently feed off the trend, that had me fast-forward in the end. It had me pay off a debt, a challenge that took me in and had me face another warning from within.

It was part of a trip down memory lane and every time I hit the end of that trend I would be on my own starting again. It was as if I was joined to the hip to those who had me face another wall. Wanting me to smash it down, so they can enter and harm me once more.

It was part of a trend that led me towards a final dead end. it was as if the only thing standing had me on the edge dramatizing about the past living in the present waiting for that waste to take effect so I can catch up and feed off the trim prim and proper effect.

It had silently crept up on me and had me face upcoming event. An expectation that had me forced to hit back with a final revelation. It had me lead the pact cause an effect and prepare myself for a force that had me face another warning at the end of that final yearning.

It was part of a second trial that had me forced to release. I was to reminisce from the trend that had me forced to start fresh. It was to create a given feast, warning me there was no presentation just a final investigation that will either make or break me if anything I hit a rude awakening.

CHAPTER 4

◆◆◆

Truth Be Told Lies Unfold

The challenge had become, silent; several on my raider ready to belt me violently. Just to break me in spirit, leave me holding a grudge hoping the end will leave me stranded. Handing the corrupt a chance to break me in spirit and haunt me while I hit back and face another united front.

The truth forced me to speak my mind; I found my way in; I took the intuitive and was forced to hit back with remorse. Only to witness the trace was part of a given, handing me a conclusion that had me fighting back by reaching my limits. All by trying to undo a conspiracy that was attached to me.

It was handing me a final, a delay that served me well along the way. It was part of a trend that held me at bay. It became part of an attentive approach every step of the way. It led me towards a journey that forced me off the edge, serving me well deserved final reservation re-training my head.

Clearing the old, starting new had me facing another final review. It was handing me a new creation to that destination. All while I continued on my path, escaped with a script that had me wonder what did I do to deserve such a serve when I hit the end of that steep thread.

The corrupt were leaving me humble but not harmed. Because I fell in a debt and a challenge that had me face another trace. It created a death threat that led me towards a journey that handed me a conclusion. It took me on a path that left me revolutionised; serving me the wrong.

It had me facing an intrigued vision, it warned me I hit a final competition; that had me fret. It was part of another trace at the end of that trend that forced me to pretend. It had me facing a final upheaval. It got to the point the corrupt were wrong but right on track; tracking me down.

For the impact had me face another trace. I had to fight back hitting the end of that trend, with a traumatic even leading me a destination that lined me up a traumatic event. I was served a debt all so I can catch up get back on track and finalise that free ride to the other side.

I hit a final a repetition that forced me to repeat and follow up on another trace. A given reason to upstage and finalise that daze that put me through a maze. It had lined me up for a key that had me finalising the trend that served me the willingness to step forward and start again.

For the corrupt hit a dead end at the end of that trend. It led me off the edge, straight into a time bomb again. Where I get in and finalise the end one day at a time. For no one believed me no one wanted to hear my side of the story. As far as they were all concerned, I was guilty.

I was stuck in the middle of a thread. Trying to piece together why I was put through vendetta. It took me in, and held me up here I was again hostage. No where to turn not aware I was locked in nowhere. No escape, just sit back and take the violation. Because the corrupt had me under wrap.

As if I had that written in my script, a challenge that served the corrupt a chance to belt me in advance. All because the corrupt took me in and made a mockery of that journey from within. A challenge that served me a failed united front, pushed me in the corner and forced me to return.

I had to break the chain and start all over again. All because my lifestyle was not worthy, it served me a yearning that handed me a warning. Now I was on the edge, trapped in the middle of a pledge. Trying to team up with he who was corrupt. Watch him fail and fall as I rise above it all.

I had to come to terms with the fact I was targeted, by those who were on my raider. They trying to convert convey and cover up another bad day. The decision of coming for me to hit me with a lie to get the truth set me free leaving them unwavering; while I surrender, hitting back with a vendetta.

What they did to get me there was warning, I was hit a terrible scare. They ganged up on me hit me with a lie then tried to cover it up with the truth. It was so turned against me I looked bad while the rest get through leaning on each other while I continue to suffer right through.

The whole concept was breached the turn of events was left to the imagination. Not only they played it with a vengeance but it gave me a fear that served me with endearment. They played it well they were calm claimant and ready to hit me with a forthcoming spell.

They won the first hand. It gave them a chance to get in the door and belt me once more. It started a fight, purely o harm me and leave broken while they continue to release peace. They took me in and faced me with a vendetta that served them well. Preventing me from repeating another spell.

Whatever I did to get to where I was had been ignored. I was not given the award I deserved I was handed a failed feast left to repeat and rebel against those who were raiding my head telepathically and trying to come up with ways to hit me run and leave me suffering in the long run.

A strategy that was done on the intention I get through that too. Then write it down and test it to he who has no freedom to see. I was faced with another feast just to claim and hand the corrupt another face to that trace. It forced me to reveal another forthcoming expense.

They used me as their muse hitting me with bad news. I was forced to hit back to get back on track. In the end I gave up, I was so badly hit emotionally lit; it left me absolutely confused. Not only the corrupt saw me as a precious stone and an easy target; there troubles had doubled.

It had confirmed the obvious, hit with an oblivion, a trace that had me face another mind reader. I was led on, taught a lesson left to repeat forced to delete. So, the corrupt can get a chance at controlling my scripture in advance. There was no time than the present to disclaim another game.

There was only a preach a challenge to help me face another trace. Even then the corrupt had no chance to return and pretend. Because the journey was cut short, the trace hit the last resort and, in the end, the only thing that stood to win; was the last thing standing.

Even then the lie had become nothing but a trend that was cut short. It forced me to hit back with remorse. So, when the time come, I could wait for the outcome to subside. For they had me up close and personal trying to come to terms with the fact I was not interested.

It was all a lie to catch me fighting back, a dead end in the end. For what it was worth and what was to come from that outcome had me stepping into the unknown. I was waiting for the right moment to declare, disclaim and follow up on another game. All I had to do Just face another final review.

For those who followed up on another scrutiny; had me stepping into the unknown. I was waiting for the corrupt to serve me a well desired choice. All so I can return and hit back and rejoice. I was taught a lesson left to repeat warned of what was to come, only to witness I hit the outcome.

With a challenge that served me well and a point taken. I was forced to fight back, it hit me with a warning, served me with a lie. It left me fighting for my life double time trying to prove I was the victim was making it worse because the corrupt already had a plan to harm me first.

What I had to do to go through hell, made me sense that the energy that served me well was passed on. It was part of a trace that had me face another given. I had to take that prediction, hand it a challenge that warned me I hit a final revelation. I went through hell serving the corrupt a spell.

All so I never get back on track and feed off that unity. I got involved in a story plot, without my knowledge I was not aware I was living a lie to give the corrupt a chance to team up on me and teach me a lesson in advance where those who knew were on the go trying to declare a final score.

I was on a path of hitting back with one more follow up;

just to get back on track. I had to make sure the corrupt never return for a nasty hit nor run. This time around its all written not misinterpreted because the corrupt hit a force that was torn and a curse that had been taken in and rehearsed.

It all back fired, right before I had a chance to state a fact. It had me fight off a demon and face that enigma that served me a final stigma. But then again, who was I to be led towards a position worse than the mission. Where my vision was impaired and my time spared. Handing me a failed attempt.

Where I was put in a position trying to get back on track and follow up on an impact. It forced me to redo and face another trace a review just so I get a claim and follow up on another game. Ready and willing to catch up and fight off that edge; God Willing. I was taken for a ride and left to subside.

Feed off the tradition that served me well from one competition to the end of that mission. It was leading me to a destination that had me forced to hit back with a repetition. It served me a well desired view, handing me the edge of reason to help me get through.

It was part of a trace that served me a given thought. It was part of a trace just to give the corrupt another crack at hitting me so they can get back on track. I was warned of the outcome a challenge that served me a well desired feast a force to help me uncover another piece.

it forced me to hit back with a challenge that had me get

back on track. I had to face a case that needed to be dealt with. For that individual who took over had freedom to gang up on me with one thought after the next for every tremor handed me a denial from that dilemma.

A troubled effect that served me a threat, hit me at the end of that forthcoming debt. It was part of a theme that had me forced to hit back in-between. It forced me to return and claim another equation to that manifestation. It served me a well desired follow up to that hold up.

The thoughts that followed took me on a path that had me face another trace. Where every thought was upcoming and every trace had me hit the forthcoming. It had me follow up on a driven ultimatum a key that served me a pure cure, from that failed unity and harm those who harmed me.

What a waste added with a haste just to turn it all around and follow up on a feast. For they had me on their raider, as an easy target. The trace had me face a driven case. A trend that served me well at every final upcoming spell. In the end of the race had faced a given; a final feast to that delay.

It forced me to repeat and regain conscious awareness again from that final bend. It had me feeding off the reading, that stopped the corrupt from repeating. It had me served another final uproar giving me a chance to return for one more glance a given reason to hit back with treason.

A final session to break the cycle had me face what was

already written. For where it begun and for what reason it served me a willingness to face what already out of place. Had me causing effects and led me to regain conscious awareness again. A will to hand me the final treason with a statement.

It served me a willingness to return and face the corrupt with a final yearning. Where every case handed me a trace. It had forced to repeat while the rest press delete. Where this time I hit the end of that tradition feeding off the corrupt and letting them in on one little secret from within.

That is when I knew there was no trial, and the trace hit me with denial. The trouble that served me well was part of a given reason to hit back with treason. Just to find a way out of that final spell. A final trap that served me well and handed me an upcoming spell.

A warning that lined me up for a yearning. Torn in more than one direction, touched by the thought not the true manifestation. For it had me reach my final destination accompanying the corrupts method with a force that will serve me well and give me a chance to sweeten the deal.

It had me face a return at the end of that theme. It brought me back to reality in between. It was part of a choice; it served me well and had me face another upcoming spell. I was left to repeat return and press delete, then when the time come remind the corrupt the outcome was a test.

It had me frail and free from that conquest. Where they

failed leaving them on the road to dire straits. no longer shall they have the power to pretend fake or false that trend nor be able to hit me again with a fake and false lead to that trace that had me face another trend.

All because that method was part of a dead end. It had me forced to hit back with an enquiry. An upcoming trend in the end that had me break the trial the error and the wonderful road that opened. It led me towards a journey unspoken. For that final review became part of a clue.

The one thing that held me up from within was last thing I expected. All because the corrupt hit me and ran and left me facing a trace to that case. It caused an effect and hit me with a dead end at the end of that trend. For what it was worth, it left me to return the favour with an outstanding event.

It was the part of a hand out where the corrupt followed up. Taken in and face an inning from within. The last thing I remembered was the first thing that come, a return to hit the corrupt with a comeback a given chance to face it all. Break the chain that entered my realm forbidden.

I was stalling just to find peace that was unravelling. it gave me an interest that was harming me from within. It had me face a hint of madness all while I wait for the corrupt to return and hit me with sadness. Handing me an emotional blackmail, was there way of pressing replay.

As if my life did not have enough to deal with, I had to accept the fact those who wanted me gone were harming me emotionally. I had faced a journey that had me spiritually and intellectually on the go. But in hindsight the feeling of neglect took over and I was left to fight back.

Leaving me waiting for the course of action to take place. Had me facing a trace that served me a willingness to hit back with a tradition at the end of that mission out of place a trace that had me forced to hit back with remorse. All by reversing the curse that had me rehearse and come first.

It caused an effect and had me forced to hit back with a death threat. I was pushed in the corner ready to face another trace. So, when the decision to break me had me faced with a turn of events had me see the road I chose was breaking the corrupts mission inevitably.

It had me burn the pages line up the curse that helped me come first. It had me on the urge ready to repeat replace and give the corrupt another chance to hit back in advance. For I was praying for a miracle to clear my name challenge the corrupt every step of the way.

All because the game was part of a lesson that served me a willingness to hit back with certainty. A message that will undo and break the silence that had me face a shining at the end of that trend. It forced me to look within and force to hit back with remorse. A follow up to the next destination.

A task, no reservation, just a key note to hit back and

follow up on a destination. A threat that set me free gave me an opportunity to reclaim my dignity. A trace to a case that gave me a second chance to hit back in advance. So, when I reached my pinnacle, I could embrace the case.

It was giving me the impression the troubles were doubled. So, when the corrupt hit me with a rumble they could return and watch me stumble. It was all prewritten and those who were in on it hired others to scheme and hit me in-between. A disheartening trap had me unravel a past test.

it had me face another quest, purely for the drama to run its course. I had to face another trace at the end of that trend. It forced me to back up and start again. The will to withstand that everlasting skill reversed back to the sender threefold handing them the energy to break the cycle.

I had to follow up on an arrival where that trial and error became part of my survival technique. I had to look within make sure those who read in-between the lines hit a dead end. Dropping it all and leaving me to portray another vision at the end of that conception to that malice.

I hit a dreadful outcome in the end. So, I don't have to put up with the lie the cheating and the constant reminder I hit a final dilemma. I realized too little to late expressing my achievements would not be rewarded. In the end I kept my mouth shut and pretended my life was ending.

It had become my reality, a final lead to the next feed. Just before I could return feed off the trial the error and the constant reminder, I hit that everlasting vendetta. When I resurrected and took the time to revive, I had to follow up on another dive. All because I failed, and fell into a prejudice rush.

CHAPTER 5

◆◆◆

Several Wanted My Attention

I had no freedom to deploy nor discuss another trace to that case. All because the corrupt were following up on a trace. It was my way of dealing with the trauma, that was handed to me when I hit the end of that trend that served me a unified front in the end.

For the corrupt had done my head in doing me harm in the long run. They caused an effect forced me off the trace hit me with a tremor and laughed at me when I hit the end of that second trial. A follow up to the next trace was a given reason to repeat replace hand the corrupt a final chapter.

Another chance to hit back in advance. It was part of a

choice that had me rejoice. a challenge that caused an effect and served me a deniable traced that served me a case. Lined up for a gift, warning me that the given trace was part of a phase that served me well and put me through hell.

It opened a door and had me follow up on a challenge once more. I was left to replace the old the new and the energy that served me right through. A strategy that caused an impression failing me an everlasting deception to that aggression that hit me with admiration.

I hit my last trial, a delay that served me a condition that tore me to bits. For the corrupt, had me on the edge, competing with whomever and trapping me like no other. I was on the edge, a compelling a trip down memory lane where I hit run and forced the corrupt to hit back in the long- run.

A charming trace was alarming, where the trend was upsetting me in the end. Where every prize was subsided and every thread was given. Where I landed had me face a driven vision that served me well at every trail and every error. A tie that was part of a given handed me a proposal.

It took me in and faced me with a disposal at every arrival; it caused an effect and failed me at every defect. For the energy that served me well had me face another upcoming spell. A Sturn effect that had me face another dead end an effect that took me in and broke me at every final whim.

Pleasing the corrupt at every forthcoming event. Made

me out to be an absolute idiot. A challenge from the past served me well and brought me forward all while I went through hell. It gave me a second chance to dive into a true reasoning just to break the cycle and hit the corrupt with treason.

An evaluation to that manifestation caused an effect and tore my heart out leaving me misjudged breaking the silence that served me well at every forthcoming spell. Interpreting every lie waiting for the corrupt to undo and follow up on another review. disguising the truth forcing my way through.

Hitting me occasionally had me attentive, where every competition made me step forward. I had to compel and comprehend every trade. A driven vision was a force that served me well at every forthcoming spell. It caused an effect and had me looking from within, trying to fight off another sin.

For what it was worth what was to come from that outcome, had no meaning. It was all part of a challenge that was brought to my attention, many years ago. Little did I know I was put in a position worse that the mission long ago. Just to give the corrupt a chance to hit me at every proposal.

A dead end, was challenging me, tormenting my ability; trying to harm my mobility. Where every time I hit a foundation a follow up, created a challenge that had me hit a final revelation. For the trace had me face another case, the freedom to repeat took me in and reported me from within.

I had to cave in on the concept, with a value to a certain key. It had me face a wonderful case. The belief that had me forced to pick on the cause had me forced to hit back with remorse. All while I pick up where I left off. So, when I reach my pinnacle the end result will become less cynical.

For the trace at the end of the race served me well, it had me face an upcoming spell. I was served an everlasting trend, heaving at me at every informal bend. Detained by the ability not the substance because the element was made up of many materialistic views.

Where every challenge had me face another bad news. I fell into a trend that caused an effect and had me face another trial and error. I fell into a heap helped myself succeed while the rest follow up on another trend. a tradition that had me forced to hit back and start again with repetition.

I had to remain silent to the game. It was part of a trace to face another given. Replace the old start new and give the corrupt an outcome with substance, nor substance to relate too. For they had no freedom nor luck to hit back because the method was too hard to face and follow up on.

I was hit with another trace at the end of that upcoming case. It forced me to fight back, prepare me for a warning; less likely for me to return to redeem a scheme in between. I had finally reached the courage to face my stalkers, only to have them gang up on me freely.

A final reality check, that took me in and faced me from

within. A trap that had me waiting for the end of that trend to force me to pretend had me face a test. while pushed off my limits all so I lose my instincts and never develop. Preparing me for the worst, where the troubles followed, come first.

For that presentation that led me towards that true reality became sinister. I was on the other end fighting a lost course and starting again. Wasting valuable time investigating a challenge that had me step in the unknown warning me the trend was a test that had me face another conquest.

I was on the edge, lead to believe the drama was part of a conquest. It handed me the second quest to that conquest. I was taught a lesson left to repeat a trace at the end of the race. Where serving me the will, will hand me a tradition that will give me a final competition to that tradition.

I was served a valuable lesson where the corrupt will pay for that too. I was ganged up on waiting for me to fail so they can sail through. It was presenting the corrupt with a challenge that had me sense I was taught a lesson left to pass a test, purely to give them a chance to cover up a trance.

A trend that ended with a forthcoming event, had me face another trace. A final freeze that led me to a break that dead end that had me face another trace. Even though a dead end at the end had me break the cycle. There was always a dead end waiting for me to return and break the cycle again.

A test that served me a silent treatment, was creating a piece. It was handing me the tradition that served me a mission convincing me otherwise. I lost my vision trying to come to terms with the fact I had a final mission courageous to state a fact a service to help me get back on track.

Delayed by the decay that served me a long-term effect of denial all the way. The trace was horrid the case was closed, the corrupt had other ideas; conspired with many trying their luck to push me off and I lose plenty. They could not wait to see if they can return for a hit run a final outcome.

For the given was part of a treason, it was leading me to confusion and the corrupt to confession. They had me trapped with a long-term effect of a winddown. A made-up story in my head, that turned heads. Even though story was part of a controversy the test became part of a conquest.

A challenge I did not follow up on, had me request. It chased me, thoroughly took me in, and fed off me wholistically from within. I had to praise give in and follow up on those who condition and face me with repetition from within. Stirring the pot, reclaiming a vision while repeating a competition.

They were preparing me for a cause and effect. Just so they can get a glimpse and a taste of another request. A worst-case scenario had come to fruition and I hit the end of my tither waiting for the corrupt to return and restore that energy on my account. They fed off me to the point I hid.

I hit a dead end that is s when I knew I had no freedom to undo nor cover up another review. An invalid challenge that restored at my own accord, had me face a trace hitting an ending that was pending. Truth be told the only way through was to undo and create a final review.

There was no tradition, it had me facing a competition. There was no challenge that had me encouraged to hit back either. What there was had me face another trace, all because the drama took over the trauma and I was stuck in a turmoil in my head. Head-spaced by a final kick off.

Fighting that demon that was placed in my peripheral vision. I was taught a valuable lesson left to return the favour and hit back with a redemption to that deception that had the corrupt forced to return for one more ungrateful mission. There was no mission worth the loss, for the gas was lit.

The trace that had me commit hit a competition. It handed to the corrupt a vision at every disposal. A chance to hit me in advance all while they were paid a commission. It had me prepared for another proposal. It led me towards a journey where I was scared to rise.

Because I was belted by those who were in disguise. Handing me a proposal that took me in and faced me with a trial and error from within. I was fed a lot of lies left to succumb another final outcome. So, when the corrupt were to return and repeat I hit a dead end and pressed delete.

It led me to dread and in the end with the same game trap that trend. Where I get in and face another inning Holding on to one more raw encore. In the end there was no praise nor a follow up to embrace a given. All because the violation was based on a final force.

It had me convinced that the challenge was untraceable. Based on a trace that served me well with every forthcoming case. It forced me to repeat replay put the corrupt through a test. Where this time they need me to reclaim review revive, following up on a theme in-between that scheme.

This time around my availability became extended. A task that left me forced to hit back with remorse. For those who needed me found a way to return and feed off me. Leaving me conditioned by a mission that had me breaking the trace and facing another violation to that manifestation.

It was not open to discussion and I was not interested in what they had to say; because it was all prewritten anyway. I was left to repeat face another feat, while prepare myself for a challenge. A journey that will lead me astray and the corrupt facing another bad day.

A true reality where this time around I gave in and wanted to break the cycle from within. I was taught a lesson left to get over it then return hurry up and feed off the drama the corrupt had achieved when they went on a rampage and created the same feed.

I was declined on every occasion, where the drama became part of a final reservation. It was part of a redemption to deny me access. Rejected at every deception unknown to man. Where I came to the realization the journey was part of a curse I could not reverse.

I was reserved for a warning hitting me at every yearning. At the end of that curve, I was pushed in the corner and forced to reclaim an internal interrogation at the end of the game. It was giving me the impression; I was led on by those who used me to declare decline and face an improvision.

A trace at the end of that tradition took over the mission. It forced me to release that beast that had me waiting for the corrupt to return and hit me with a challenge that lined me up for a threat. It had me sweat in dirt lining me up for a cleanse that forced me to redo release and break another feast.

I could not see why I was pointed and left to hit back anointed. Seen as I was brought forward by the corrupt to hit me and run leading me to a destination that had me face a curse at the end of that verse. For the corrupt were to return and face me with an interest torn in more than one direction.

Leaving me forced to hit back with a vision had me face an interrogation. Forming a mission that failed me at every investigation. It had me sponsored by the wrong purely there to break me and feed off the tradition. It served me a willingness to break that trend, that hit me with a dead end.

It was giving me the impression I hit the end of that trend, that forced me to give in and start fresh then again. Handing the corrupt a final release from that feast that had me redeem another scheme. It had me reaping a reward at the end of that classification.

A rude awakening from that mission taught me a valuable lesson. I was truly taken for a ride it had me face a warning from that final yearning. It gave me a respite to that trade that had me forced to hit back in spite of what was meant to be. Even though the drama was already thought over.

I took the initiative decline an indicative trace. For the trend was too hard to compete compel and uncomprehend. I had to Create a piece extend that feast, release and prepare myself for a brand-new feast. Meanwhile give in and feed off the drama set aside from within.

I was to give in, set the gaol, then hand it to next bystander. Apparently, my light was not strong enough to remain bright. They brightened my day when I reached my pinnacle resent me and belted me every step of the way. He who had made his mark simply decided to side with the wrong tribe.

Meanwhile, the corrupt took me in and divided into two sections. A world less likely to heave and a challenge that had me face another contamination to that manifestation. It led me to believe I was nowhere near I was meant to be. Led on, left to break the chain while the rest remain silent.

It was giving me the impression I hit a deception from

that failed manifestation. I was causing effects trapped in the middle of a defect. I had to accept defeat, all while I watched the corrupt feed off the tribe that served me a complaint. A trace to help me replace the old the new and the upcoming clue.

I was trying my luck to not enter that realm, but it was hitting the corrupt with a final countdown. An entrapment that served me a treat. Where it took me down and mentally served me well. All while I hit a home run and face another trick that had me hit a trip down memory lane.

It had me forced to hit back with remorse, for that energy was to return for a second trial. It was causing effects raiding my head so I never resurrect. It had me remain the same lining me up for a challenge that forced me to create a trap. I was hit with an entity reminding me I had no freedom.

What I had was the lack of energy to sustain that liability. I was put in a position worse than I could imagine. Because I had an enemy who wanted to use me to make it happen. For the corrupt, hit me continuously, forced me to repeat and repel. Gaining wisdom while putting me through hell.

I was pushed in the corner and literally driven towards insanity. Just to give the corrupt a chance to hit me with an entrance that took its toll. Forced to let go and follow up on a no show. A given reason to hit back with one more chance to break the cycle in advance; all while I remain holy.

Even though it was proven and the test was over written. The trace was part of an addiction that led me towards a journey that brought me forward. Forced me to return and hit back with a vision. Where thy tried to get me elicited, for their own safety. Hitting an end of a task I facing a dead end.

All it did was leave me hitting a hold up; on the hope they hurry it all up. For the journey was not working in unison with those who had me sitting pretty. Waiting for the cause an effect to break the system covering up another conviction. A condition that hit me at every possibility.

I was not to blame, the corrupt were on their way; anyway, playing it their way. I was their victim; I was taken for a fool, thrown off edge. All on the hope I lose my mind and the corrupt return to pledge. Assuming they had all the answers in their vision, where every jurisdiction played a part.

They had me locked in while keeping me close up and personal; attempting to break my vibe. A pledge that backfired, and blackened that circle of events that had me withstanding another given request. In hindsight I lost my peripheral vision, trying to make do and sense of my reality.

It became part of a proposal, that left them turning the pages and going insane. Lining me up for one more return. Causing the right effects testing the pages and creating a piece so I can resurrect. I fell into a rut, where it took me in forced me to catch up and break the corrupts wing. What an ending!

The assumption I was there, purely to save them, was pausing effects. It no longer served its purpose. It was part of a vision where I broke the silence. It forced them to hit back watching them all turn against each other as I get back on track. A trap, no longer; for the invasion was infrequent.

CHAPTER 6

◆ ◆ ◆

A Rumour Released A Riot

They lost me at every trace, where I was given a reason to return and follow up on a trial and error and a final vendetta. Warned of what was to come from that upcoming outcome. I was to hit back with one more given theme, a scheme that had me forced to face a trial-and-error in-between.

I was belted by the corrupt, silently taken over, forced to free myself. A challenge that had me live in doubt. Try my luck to return, face a trace at the end of that forthcoming case. For they attempted several hits before that stated a fact. Accused abused and left me stepping into bad news.

Where I was cornered, left to question their motives. For those who knew had released that beast to determine what angle will hand them a final theme. It will help them scheme in-between. Forcing me to face my true reality. It restored the corrupts method leaving me causing the wrong effects.

It had me on the move, humble ready to scheme. Realizing the drama was too hard to redeem. It had me face an easy case just to replace another trace. A given reason to return and help the corrupt hit me with foul play so they can return and press replay

All while the rest found an opportunity to twist those words around. Purely to force me to give in and harm me instantly with a whole lot of animosity. I was left to repeat from within then return to attempt to feed off that beast. It had me forced to hit back with my mind back on track.

I was consciously aware, it stirred the pot, left me to rot. It forced me to overdo another review. They hid that spell well and decided to try their luck and harm me periodically. All by attempting to hand me bad luck. Stirring the pot, forcing me to repeat, delete delay and press replay.

Faced with a given case, handed a clue and left to pick up where I left off. Just to clear the old and start new. I was to face another final review, a given a chance to hit back for no reason. It handed me a proposal that claimed my truth. I was catch up feed off the trend that had me face a dead-end.

My method was used against me, just so they can return and attempt to steal another key. This time around I was willing and able to give in to that cable. For the condition was bleak and I was on the edge of breaking the cycle with a competition that will leave me sacred.

For the corrupt were hitting a holdup. It had me step into the unknown a conquest that had me reprieve and achieve a forthcoming goal. It served me wonders and put me through a trial and error and final vendetta. What had become part of a clueless outcome, had achieved a dream.

It had me on the receiver end trying to achieve another goal in-between. It had me restoring my received by the truth that had me face another trace at the end of the race. In the end the only drama standing by my side was the trace that failed me back then; feeding off the debris.

So, when the time come, I could create an entrance to serve the corrupt a final vengeance. It had me create a trace towards a journey that forced me to repeat, replace and cover up another trick to that trade. For they were using me to overcome an outcome they concocted to come out innocent.

Meanwhile, I took the chance, hit the corrupt back in advance. Prayed for a miracle so I can continue to repeat and repel against those who took me in and put me through hell. I was given a chance to hit back in advance forced to rerelease that time bomb that had me face another feast.

I caught up fell into a trace trapped in the middle of a

case. Then when the time come try my best to overcome another conquest. Cleanse with a trap, that had me forced to hit back an overlay of another bad day. The troubles were a treat a trend became part of a siren that hit me with silence.

I was to blame for every upcoming claim, for apparently, I rising above that game brought them shame. Driving me insane was the corrupts way of pushing me off the edge. Where they attempted to repeat repel and face me with an upcoming spell. What a claim that had me face another trend.

Where every journey had me return for a yearning. Where everything that served me well from within gave me a chance to return for another chance to get in and win. But what I was meant to win was a true rude awakening. A challenge that had me see I had no luck, and the freedom to be.

What they handed to me was not as rewarding as it was meant to be. For the corrupt were handing me a chance to rise above that fall feeding off the trend that served me a well desired trap. For I was given a them to break the chain that led me to force up and face the corrupt once again.

In the end of that overhaul the call back was not as easy as it was meant to be. The wall collapsed handing me a second chance to face another trace and feed off the system at the end of that case. I was given a reason to pick on the corrupt with a final trace at the end of the race.

All while the rest were attempting to harm my success.

They were on the edge, raiding my head hoping every term works against me. They return at every form, hitting me and running attempting to break me at every forthcoming. Trapping me against my free will, tearing my heart out.

I sat in the corner, alone no support, just the knives embedded in my back. Where the corrupt conspired against my free will just to break me apart so I fall apart. Reaching my potential was part of a trend that had me feel that I had no freedom my foundation was again being torn.

My words torn twisted my trend hitting a dead end and the only way to accept defeat was hit back and to start fresh while I remain silent from within. My heart was not in the right place and the only way to deal with the down fall was given in not look back and let them in.

Making me out to be a fabricator, warned the corrupt to stand low. Where the only thing that had me forced to get in was the trace that led me towards a journey that had stay away while the rest pressed replay. They had me on trial served a key an error handing me a final vendetta.

There were several on my raider getting in and breaking the system from within. As if I was left to break that trade that forced to return and follow up on a journey that became too hard to repeat beat the buzzer too easy to press delete, way to honest to undo and follow up on a review.

They made me out to be a fabricator; carelessly not give a damn. For I was led to believe I was part of the dream. Bu the dream became a nightmare in between. A scam was part of a scheme that handed the corrupt a theme in-between. I became bait, at every trial and error.

It forced the corrupt to push me off the edge and hand them a concept, that trapped me in the end. It led me to believe, that every trace had me face another case. Giving me the impression every journey had me face another admission. Hated by many admired by most causing effect.

All while the rest, harm me at my every conquest. It was meant to cause an effect and have me face another detection to that redemption. A trend that had me fail then try my luck while I continue to repeat another redemption to that deception it had me cause an effect and break the cycle.

Trapping those who were given a reason to repeat and follow up on another trace at the end of the race. It gave me an attempt to restore what I thought was the last resort. All so I can never get in unless I give in so when I do get in the trial becomes part of an error final endeavour.

It forced the corrupt off the edge and handed me a vendetta. It was based on a given, a chance to hit back with a phase that had me face another case trapping those who endeavour to devour and face me with a final empowerment. Leaning towards helping themselves while I face a dead threat.

I had no reservation, no chance to build around that final destination. I was hit with another trace at the end of that race. I was warned of what was to come from that outcome. A treason that had me face another trace that served me. I was served, a well desired and final trend.

According to the corrupt I could not see. Blind as a bat trying to catch up and get back on track. Where that feast that was covering up another trace that could not undo fast enough. I had to return and desire a new thread of redemption. What I had to do just to find peace was creative.

I had no chance in hell of creating a dead end at the end of that final return. I was taught a lesson left to redeem a scheme for I had rude awakening in between. A chance to return to face a trace and feed off the redemption that had me face a tradition towards that final repetition.

I was accompanied by the last thing that had me face an entrance from within. It served me a release from that final beast. A chance where I get in and bless that tradition handing the corrupt a final repetition. I was taught a lesson left to repeat taken for a fool. Without ever creating a piece.

I was pushed in the corner to rule out the least expectation to that mission. For what I thought was the everlasting feast, became part of a final recognition to the mission. It had me face a trace ready to hit back with denial. A composition at the end of that mission became apparent.

I was left to hit back with a trace to serve me well at the end of the race. I had no freedom nor foundation to sweeten the deal. For what I knew and for what was meant to be true was the last thing on my mind and the first thing that had me forced to get in from the last thing standing.

I was hit with a vision creating a trace towards a final composition. The proposal was a lie to bring me forth then push me off the edge so I never catch up or even follow up on a trend, that was to serve me well in the end. It was purely to ruin my me, dim my light and leave me suffering silence.

All so I never catch up, or even create a piece that will give me peace. I was forced to hit back with a vengeance. Lining me up for a curse that had me return for one more verse. When I reached the peak in the end; I was hitting the air. It became a consistent reminder that the trace was invalid.

I had come to the conclusion I was facing another confusion. That's when I realized I was being entertained by those who wanted a piece of the action. It was part of a vision that had given me the impression the journey was about to hit a hold up. I hit a turning point trying to get out of a sin.

Waiting for the corrupt to condition the mission and change that consistency from within. Led me to believe there was no thought in the whole pattern because the journey was too hard to conceive. For they had me forced to reveal an everlasting concept waiting for me to fail.

All so the corrupt can continue on their journey and sail. With the intention they get in harm me from within slow down and hit me with redemption from the beginning to the end holding me to ransom so they can restart and face me with a trauma that had me forced to hit back with an aroma.

It had me facing a violation, to that manifestation. I was causing effects ever so lightly, hoping everything will fall into place; the corrupt decline every trace. The trial and error ended that dilemma unravelling another trend that will derive and hand me a witness from hell.

Giving me a second chance to face another trance. Where that final investigation will lead me off track preparing for a new clue. A challenge that will help me get through. It was part of a case that handed me a given and prepared me for a dead end in the end haunting me at every trend.

On one occasion to the next destination, I was left to reminisce a past contradiction. A contrast between the edge of reason, where Every test became a contest, and a kind way to accept defeat. A conquest that had me face another conflict, where I was hit and left running from that kick.

I was pushed off the edge of that forthcoming event. Where the energy that surrounded me faced me with a key. It was part of a trap at the end of that contract. It lined me up for the wrong end of that trend. It had me warned I hit a dead end. Locking me in trapping those who use me to get in.

It opened a can of worms a treasure chest fool of maggots. As if it was coffin and something was buried deep inside. Where I connected the dots and realized to little too late to my own oppression I open pandoras box and all the lies come alive. Heaving at me trying to kindly continue to harm me.

I gave in and moved on; I had no idea how I come across too many who saw me easy. For those who wanted to lend a helping hand harmed me; after the fact. Then tried to cover it up by proving that fact. As if I was hit with a challenge, a degree of tricks that had me face another given scene.

Where in the end, that train of thought; caused an effect. It created an obscene theme at the end of that final scheme. A tradition that had me release a feast hitting back with a cause an effect. Warning me I was way too hard on myself and the only way out was to silently take it all in.

Move forward once again, pray to God I get heard. For those who used me to get through, never see light. nor even have the power to give in fight and harm me from within. I had to face that scene that made me see I was heaving wasting energy looking from within; praying for all of it to end.

Continuing on my journey had me carrying a flame that served its purpose right before hit the end of that upcoming game. It had me stepping into a trace that served in hell. Ending the race and pushing me in the corner assuming the choices were made were decided by he who knew.

It was presenting me with a forthcoming event. Where I had to come to terms with the facts. I was turned my words twisted, and everything worked in unison with one counterpart. A reaction handing me an abreaction. I was on the move waiting for a trace to give in and hand me a win.

I was led on counting the days, as if I was living in a daze. Outnumbered feeling trapped no longer living on a positive vibe. Because those who knew were on my raider waiting patiently for the day, I give in so they can return and press replay from within. Hoping I lose my head trying to look ahead.

I had nowhere to turn, no outlook to overturn, just an outcome that handed me destruction. The corrupt made sure I hit the lowest point so when I reach that minor feast the only thing that served me well from with. It was the enigma that handed me that stigma in the end of that trend.

Purely on a given, standing ovation, so I never get back up, get back on track or even feed off the tread. Because I was led to believe that the drama was too hard to perceive. If I had left it to chance when the time had come, the outcome would end up less likely for me to relive a nightmare.

It was all done, set up by the corrupt, purely to push me in the corner so I give up. They handed me them an entrance to an outcome that took me in and faced me with the demon who wanted to keep feeding off me from within. It would have become something out of the ordinary.

But in hindsight it handed me a logic that will serve me well in the long run. It gave the corrupt a given opportunity to release that beast. Then when the time come hit back serving me a long-term effect of terror that left me hitting back with a total dilemma.

I found myself in a position worse than the mission. Less likely to case that trace that served me warning a well-deserved yearning, at the end of the race. For the challenge would leave me hunting for a feast. It took me on a journey that had me hit an ending that was cunning.

A trip down memory breaking the cycle. A trial that was never meant to be for me, but apparently, I was used abused on purpose. It made no sense of the accusations the manipulation was part of an assimilation. A constant reminder I hit a pathfinder. Left to suffer while the corrupt prosper.

For they were giving me a chance to release that demonic feast. The one that had me portray another dead end. It was handing me the inclusion to fit in and hit a final delusion. I gave in and handed the corrupt a chance to release that beast and face another trace at the end of the race.

I was about to lose my light, my dignity and the last draw just before I hit an encore. I was trying to get in and fight my way through only to witness I hit the end of that trend that forced me to repeat repel and start again. A link distracting that friction, where I determine the outcome.

A reification had come to fruition. handing the corrupt a dead end to that manifestation. My faith in humanity failed immensely. It took me in with the last thing that trapped me from within. I had to face another trace look forward not back then when the time come overcome that outcome.

CHAPTER 7

◆ ◆ ◆

I Think I Hit Seventh Heaven, Yet Again; Amen

Every challenge that I met with, I was to repeat and follow up on a treat. There was always a momentum that had me step into a trace that had me face an upcoming case. What I knew and what was to come from that overview, there was always a chance, no return for one more trance.

For that reason, I was handed a bad omen, repeating a bad day. The vision I once knew had me questioning every final review. I was now lined up for a trace that had me hit the end of the race. It had become a faith less likely for me to erase. The journey I was on was, help me move on.

Even though I was left to repeat there was always a part that led me to depart. A part of me that harmed the corrupt and led me towards a journey that made me give up. The rough took over, the trough, and the given had me run for a trace that served me a dead end at the end of the race.

A trend that lined me up for a dead end, became a lie. It gave me a second chance to get by. I was warned, and the only thing that had me waiting for the end to begin was the last thing standing. For I was given a chance to repeat repel and face a trace; a given reason to hit back with treason.

There was no key, no trial not even an error just a final vendetta. I was to give in and hand the corrupt a given chance to hit back in advance. When I reach my peak, the only thing standing was the journey that was everlasting. It was part of a task that gave handing me a true rude awakening.

It had me on the corrupts raider, a trace that had me wonder off. An energy that had me face another season. I had to return and hit back with treason. Where I was given a gift that kept me aligned. It was leading the blind and leaving me speaking my mind.

Even though I was left behind I was taught a lesson. Traumatised by the past living in the present. Lining myself up for another trace at the end of that trend that had me forced to let go and start again. I was taken for a fool. Lined up for a challenge that me return for another yearning.

Working towards a trip down memory lane had me face another game. About to gamble my life away, a given reason to release that beast. It had me face another feast. I was taken for a ride, left to repeat a line up for another day then state a fact create peace and follow up on another feast.

A trace at the end of the race was praised. It gave me a presentation to follow up on another destination. I was taken for a ride taught and left to release that beast that had me forced to hit back. All while I continue to get back on track and undo every clue periodically.

I was led on, let down and left to state facts on my own. No chance was given; I was left to undo every trace spaced out with total doubt. As I reach my peak the only thing left standing was the last thing that had me forced to hit back with remorse; withstanding another cause.

I was on a path of admiration, but well into a journey of repeating. I was lifting up my spirit where I fell into a deep silent interrogation. I was hit with a vengeance no longer feeling as inadequate it was all mainstream. I had to return repeat and remain serene while I catch up and another feat.

Where the instigation became worrisome and the trace untorn. The truth had me set free, but in what category; only time could tell. All I knew is I went through hell, fighting off those who were on my raider causing effects. Leaving me suffering in silence all while the rest hit me with an alliance.

I was turning heads; it left me hitting a hold up because of it. I was torn in more than one direction; it had me state facts face my true reality. It was giving the corrupt a chance to set a time a date and failed attempt to hit me with a force that served me well at the end of that spell.

All while the rest were on my raider forcing me to hit back; like I was the perpetrator. I was trapped in the middle of a riddle; blamed for everything that went wrong. It left me wasting energy trying to break free. When truly I was meant to let go, without having to face an unwanted catastrophe.

The anguish that I carried left me to undo and follow up on another clue. So, when I reach up to that level, I felt trapped no trace to overlap. It had me fail and face another trial, all while I was tearing pages testing the waters and trying my luck to return and face another unwanted invalid sacrament.

I was left to return and hit back with a line up. Restoring my energy and reviving a constant reminder I hit a hold up a challenge that had me see I was nowhere near the corrupt final hold up. I was to catch up, hunt down and follow up on a pinnacle; only to witness the hint became serious.

There was trick to that trace, I was handed a trick that invaded my space. It was all part of a given just to hand me a feeling I hit the energy that served me a rude awakening. For every thought that took me in, scored me a goal and belted me from within. Waiting for me to lose every thought.

Even the part that hit me within the last resort. For every unwanted thought had me hit back and face another trace. Hinting to me I had no foundation to replace, no lead to endeavour, just a follow up to the next presentation a lead that will hand me a final manifestation.

Preparing me for the worst, was handing me a key to reverse. All while I get in revert to the next inning. The corrupt no longer have the power to break the cycle a lead towards a final. For next destination had me face a foundation. Waiting for that key to give me a chance to get in.

Where I was faced with a true reality from within. All so they can win an upcoming event. Reassuring me they were torn and they will leave me alone so I can continue to roam. Assuming they had the power to vent. Where each follow up took me closer than before, facing me with an encore.

Where I had to power through, and face me with a reality check. For the divinity to that second trial had me forced to hit back with remorse. It was handing me the vibe that had me face another dive. Where everything that was meant to come to fruition; had me facing another interrogation.

Where my intuition kicked in and forced me to hit back from within; rounding it up to one more sin. For the corrupt were interrogating me at every destination. A path that was not so profound, actually the sound was twice as hard and the vibe took me on a path to help me remain alive.

I was left to pretend all while the corrupt were planning another hit and run. The trend was pending the trap was never ending the method was opaque and the journey from within was beginning to look opaque. Even though the trace had me victimised, I felt paralysed from within.

Sterilizing that sin, that had me forced to hit back with remorse. The one sin that had me forced to give in, faced me with a trial an error and a final vendetta. I had my faith tested my vision reversed, so when I hit the end of that trend, I was no longer cursed. Victimised by those who knew.

For those who knew wanted to hire others to gang up on me too. It became a lottery ticket; many were buying it assuming they would get me down and harm me periodically. I was torn in more than one direction trying to reclaim and face another trend that had me begging for mercy in the end.

All I could sense was who was in on it, and when were they to return for the next hit. They were giving me hard time waiting for me to sail through and feed off the trace that had me face another clue. The trend became evil the trace had me face another trip down memory lane.

I was given a reason to undo and follow up on a treason right through. The given response, was a given reason, it was to hit back with a harsh reality. For the faith I was handed, was branded. I was on remand waiting for name to be cleared while corrupt accept a bribe hoping his method will stay.

In fact, all it did was stir the pot, hit me with a vengeance; so, I never catch up. I was constantly fed off, trapped in the middle, where the trace was always corrupt. I just could not accept the road I was on, it handed me a final vendetta, to remain strong. Because the journey I chose was always morose.

I was taken for a fool, branded left stagnant to my development. A given a test, a powerful progress. It had me follow up on a dream where in the end face another trace handing me to the resolution to fight back a rude awakening. To revolutionise what I thought was the beginning of an end.

On the hope I give in and face that trace that was pending from within. I had been served a well-deserved desire where he was stalking me had been on my raider for way too long. His obsession had become part of a condition that had me weighed down and lined up for a bad ending.

Just because he was corrupt, way too eager to rise above. I was trapped in middle of a terrible lie it had me face another trace serving me a failed attempt handing me the power to redo replace and follow up on a case where everything I did became his freedom to return and hit me with Logistics.

I was left to remain silent, the where strategy they used in the end they had no choice but to vandalise my property break my nerves and attempt to return and harm me in the long term. All while he who was stalking my existence. Serving me a trace that had me foreclose another phase.

It had me return feed of the case then when I least expect it force it all to erase. It had me on the edge trapped in the middle of a forthcoming riddle. Where every turn served me a loyal test and presented me with a final request facing me with a final conquest to that creative feast.

For the journey I was on had me entertained with the thought that served me wrong it forced me off the edge leading me to a destination that took me on a journey that faced me with a true reality. It gave me a trace ready and willing to hit back God willing. That is when I knew no point was taken.

I had no freedom to repeat, no trust in humanity to press delete. All I had left was my conscious awareness up and going ready to catch the corrupt confess. Where I was nowhere near the corrupts final fear, if anything I was taught a lesson left to hit back with a reason.

Where the treason, became an expense to close one door and open another flaw. It was a challenge that become an entertainment where the truth served me well it gave me a chance to return for one more key. Where the proof was insightful and the challenge hindered by the truth.

I was hunted down, forced to rewrite my destiny. Where

every angle gave me a chance to hit back with a substantial amount of at pride. It was giving me an opportunity to break the trend and face the case a given reason to break the silence and feed off the treason.

It had me trace that trend the led me down the path of creating a trial an error in the end. It was a final vendetta a challenge that served me well it had me face another upcoming spell. It was part of a given, a pass event that had me release that beast that caused the wrong effects.

It had me face a tranquil event, that had me forced to vent. It had me focused on a passageway that served me a well. A desired foundation that lined me up for a curse that forced me to hit back with a verse. A recreation to that manifestation that brought me forward and gave me a final destination.

A challenge that brought forward led me to rehearse; I was given a chance to hit back in advance. I had no remorse nor the courage to return for another cause and effect. I had to rehearse and find a way to serve me well and face me with another ongoing spell.

It gave me a chance to hit back with a curse, that served me well at the end of that verse. The energy that had me on the go moved me, moved on and left wondering what did I do wrong. It served me a trace, that led me to erase another forthcoming case.

It was preventing me from repeating and reliving that trend. It served me well intended intervention that forced me to repeat, hit back and press delete. All while

I delay and deny the corrupt access the way, where the end of that trend was a given. The beginning of a task that served me a bad omen.

A caution to the wind served me a trade, that is when I knew I hit a contest. It was about to cave in on me. Leave me bombarded with a whole lot of energy. It had me repeat repel and push me in the corner forcing me to restore my energy periodically. Freeing me from a task not worth approaching.

It had me face another given reason to hit back and feed off the trace. It was hinting to me I hit the end of that race with one upcoming key. An event that served me a challenge that stalled handing me a well and troubled spell. It forced me to repeat replace and face another case.

For the energy that served me well took over my spirit and put me through hell. For whatever was said or done, I had no freedom to overcome that outcome. I had to face another trace, follow up on another given disgrace. All while the corrupt cut my life support hoping I would not resuscitate.

Cutting the cord, so I don't recite the lie, had me on standby. It was perishing the corrupts method handing them a second chance to dive into a given trace. It was forcing me to hit back with a final case. Making sure I have no leg room, no leg to stand on so they could continue to break my spirit.

A cheap shot was to come my way, where every journey

served me a yearning. It caused an effect and had me face a rejection. I was sabotaged in the long run, the dream of creating a piece to give me peace ended up a nightmare in-between. I was left suffering in silence for I was laughed at.

I had nowhere to turn no freedom to return. What I had was a given, a gift that kept me honest, I lost my thought pattern it was as if someone took over my head and tried so impatiently to report me and push me off the edge. I was trapped in the middle of a forthcoming event.

It was preventing me from reliving my destiny, I had to unfold every child hood story untold. A dream that had me on the edge, trapped trying to make it happen but those who knew the story plot could not wat to break me so I never reach it. Left to repeat and follow up on another treat.

So, when I caught up, I could repeat repel and follow up on another spell. For those who knew could not wait to break me and feed off me right through. It was part of a scam that had me once again ashamed to fight back. I could not release another positive piece; where it took over my peace.

The trauma took over; it had me facing another win. I was praised, taken for granted left to chance fell in a spiral. Into a world that was nowhere near I was meant to be. There was always a drama that took over and I was left to release that demon before it became part of the corrupts final game.

It had me forced to hit back with remorse. There was no freedom or faith every waking moment had me hit a final trace. The tradition that forced me to hit back with repetition, it lined me up for lineage. No trace given no temperament reviewed, just an outcome that had me face another step.

It was all prewritten, the drama the trace the given permission for me to repeat and replace. I missed the boat all because the corrupt saw me better as a remote. The step forward had me look back there was no reminder no trace to replace. Just a given trend that had me forced to pretend.

All while I gave in and faced another dead end. Tapping into another true rude awakening. I had no freedom no friendships to lead me towards a journey to give me hope. What I had was a lead to hand me a final breed serving me the trace that took me on a journey that forced me to release.

I had repeat replace and press delete. For what I had and for what it was worth the journey was a curse. It was purely for me to come first last and hit a dead end. Chewing on a bone that will always serve me wrong. It had me pretend that every thought was part of a forethought.

It was basically a challenge that had me return and face another given. Where every thought took me in and faced me with a trial and error a final delay added with a dilemma. It had me sense I hit a free ride to the other side hitting the corrupt with a challenge that had me erase that case.

The corrupt had returned and faced me with a missile. A dirty trick to serve me unwell so when I hit the end of that strategy I'm left in tragedy. My light had dimmed my journey was trapped, the only thing left was to pass a test and watch my trace erase. Leaving me on the edge strapped for thought.

All so the corrupt can undo upstage and harm me right through. It served me well for what had me forced to hit back was following up on a key that served me and pushed me off track. I was waiting for the truth to set me free. For the spiral effect had me forced to hit back with a unified trend.

CHAPTER 8

◆ ◆ ◆

I Fell Into A Dream Where The Drama Heaved

An interaction with a debt had me fail every thread. May the curse reverse the trace embrace and that trend that hit me at the end, find its way through. Where I was searching for an interest that was part of a binding contract. It handed me a challenge that served me a key.

Running the risk of becoming alienated, had me face another trace. Handing me the tradition to catch up ad follow up on another vision. All by reading between the lines and trying my luck to face another trace and feed off the trip that had me forced to hit back with remorse

A system that was part of the mission had relapsed. It never made it until the end there was a challenge that served me a will to reserve the right to follow up and hit back with an all-mighty big bang theory. The old fight became the new, and the beginning had me facing another review.

It forced me to bruise, badger and break that ledger. For every journey that was written it had me rubbed raw constantly trying to get out of that wrong road only to realize I ended it periodically with a journey that had me pausing effects. While being published in many formations.

It had me on the cusp ready and willing to combust. Where everything hit; I had physical pain, public ridicule I even ended up pausing effects just to find peace at the end of that feast. A challenge that had me forced to hit back and leave it all to chance. A test that was pending had resurrected.

I was left certain, that every dream was worse than the curse. It had me face another verse it. I became, cynical repeating a trip down memory lane. About to be pushed off the edge and drive me insane. Taught a lesson left to the imagination, where every thought made me see the light.

I was to let it go, set it free step into a shock mode all by returning and feeding off the trace that had me on the go. Ready to respond to every feast. Where the cause an effect faced me with a light at the end of the tunnel. It stirred the pot locked it in and watched the corrupt rot from within

It gave me a second chance to restore my energy and feed off me in advance. I had to serve another reserve. Waste my time waiting for the journey to face a trace at the end of the case. It had me step into an entrance that forced me to reveal a test. Just to hand the me a quest at the end of that race.

It had me on the role and the corrupt ganging up on me facing a final degree. It had me reprimanded and presenting the corrupt with a chance to hit back in advance. It was part of a verse that had me forced to hit back. Then when the time come face another given so the corrupt break the trace.

It handed me a first and an everlasting key, a prewarning that served me a yearning. I was stalling holding on to a rude awakening, it had me face a trace where every thought forced me to hit with remorse. It left me to pretend portray face a trace and feed off the concept that tore me to bits.

I was on the road to repeat, replace and face a trace. Where I was given a reason to pass a test, push forward and progress. For no one really knew how to push me off the edge, and no one had a clue, for what was to come from that outcome was an extension to that redemption.

It had me face a treason and those who thought they knew me hit back with a final review. Handing me the outcome I needed to catch up and screw them too. I was taught a lesson left to repeat where every thought hit me with the last resort a treason to reclaim another trace that served me well.

All so when I caught, I could easily face another reason to follow up on a kind heart. I was given a break to face another case only to witness I hit an eye witness. It had me face what I thought would be part of a creative trace, it had me forced to endower and break apart.

All while I feed of the empowerment. I could not release that beast that had me undo and follow up on another review. I had to face another feast on the condition I repeat another repetition. All so the corrupt can praise that phase that served me a well desired and deserved praise.

Those who had freedom to play it could return and serve me a strain. A string of events that took me in and brought me tension from within. It forced me to repeat and rebel against those who used me to see beyond and face me with a true reality. A failed attempt to hit me from within.

All because serving me well, was to help me lead and succeed while I move forward. But all it did was hand me a clue all while they attempt to win and face another treason from within. I was connecting to the faith that served me a warning and handed me a trend at the end of that yearning.

I was left to relive and face another reason to bounce back and force the corrupt off the edge. For they took me on pathway that had me leading me off the edge starting fresh. I had to face another trend at the end of that forthcoming event. It became a free ride in the end where I get a break.

My journey hit me with a yearning, it forced me to redo a challenge. I had to pretend and repeat a brand-new given theme. It had me trace a praise where those who haunted me in the past were living in the present confronting me with another cast. It had me facing the true meaning in the end.

A failed attempt to break the trend. For the corrupt were planning another hit, a seed to the midst was planted before I had a chance to hit back in advance. Hoping I would fail and fall for that too. All it did was have me face another trend that led towards a level of abundance; a future resistance.

A trace that trapped me in the middle of a cave; where I entered a coven. It was a journey that had me locked in, waiting for the corrupt to harm me whenever they got a chance to hit me with weak spot within. Assuming I had one more thing I had to gather from within.

In true fact what I had was a challenge to teach me a lesson to get back on track. They saw me as an easy target. In fact, they were feeding that seed that they planted long before they took me for granted. They had me on the go chasing dreams that ended up becoming a nightmare in-between.

That is when I knew I was grounded; I could not rise nor even overcome an outcome. They saw me as an easy target, trapped me in the middle of that havoc. Reserved the right to return for respite. I was warned of what was to come, so when I reached my pinnacle, I could undo that review.

Where the only thing that had me facing a trace from within was running thin. The lining was over powering; the trace had me face a trend. So, when I reached my pinnacle, I could undo look forward and start again facing another trail error and a final vendetta.

I had given it a minute, before I was left to restore that last given encore. I had to release then when the time come overcome another trial error with a final vendetta. Because the clock was ticking and the drama had me overwhelmed there was a trace that served me an indifference.

It gave me the power to undo and devour. I was poisoned by the truth left to suffer in denial so when I reach my peak the corrupt can return repeat push me in the corner and press delete. Not this time around the only thing they had left was to sit and wait then hand me love not hate.

They had no fight left in them, what they had was a conspiracy to return and try to convince me otherwise. The lie took over the truth that challenge had me forced to hit back with remorse so when the time come, I could redo and follow up on another review.

I was given a presentation had me facing a trauma. As if the dream had me forced to hit back in-between. For the conviction to hand me another competition became part of the vision. Not only I was left to suffer in silence but I was put in a position that had me face another competitor.

Where I entered freely completed a task, took over that journey that had me face another trace. A trial an and a follow up to the next vendetta. It had me at every proposition handing the corrupt a dead end at the end of that vision. Not only I was taught a lesson but I was left hitting a contest.

It had me stepping into the unknown warned of what was to come from that outcome. It served me a clue. It caused an effect and broke the chain all while I went through it all and created a brand-new game. Where I became a visionary to that competition just to claim that game.

It had me on the edge, ready to pledge claim my truth and face another given. Just to face my reality because I was hit with a final forced to hit back with denial just to find peace at every final. before I was about to enter there was another hit and the corrupt were ready to hit me with a ledger.

As if my journal, was not hard enough to bare. The burden to undo the chaos in my head raised me from the dead. I carried that crucifixion straight to the end of my trial and conviction. It gave me stigmata and a second chance to divide conquer and face another treason.

That trace that served me the will to replace. Not only led me to believe that the drama had me troubled ready to replay. But the curse had me on the edge, ready and willing to repeat. I had to replace that warning with a dream. It had me facing a follow up in between.

I was left to return and break that trend that served me a well-balanced dead end. I was not able to state my facts without allowing the corrupt to catch up nor get back on track. Trapped me in the middle of a forthcoming riddle. It had me thorough ready to hit back with drama.

I was to let it all go, set it all free, accept my faults and pretend it was all a dead end. but I had others judging my existence, trying their luck to return and hitting me with a bad omen. In the end I gave in on the condition I fought back and win every mission.

Leaving them living in denial, all while I was on my way of accepting defeat. It made me see I was no longer repeating the same intriguing game. For this time around I found another way to repeat and finalise that method that had me forced to press delete. I was working on a trace to hand me a case.

A proposition to lead me to the next competition was irrelevant. Lining the corrupt up for a failed vision had me stepping into the unknown waiting for the corrupt to return for another final endeavour. It had me on the edge reasoning with the devil, just to claim another trial and error.

What a waste of time, I was facing a challenge a test of endurance. For what I thought was the last resort, was basically a bully attack ready and willing to declare disclaim and follow up on another game. Once again bring shame to my name. Handing them a chance to repeat and remain the same.

Where royalty ended up becoming disloyalty. Where every trace took over the drama and left me second guessing. I was hitting a royal flush just to save myself for another crush. A final vendetta where they became forced to hit back creating a piece from an informal validation.

Confirming the obvious, was a game that had me remain the same. I was about to gamble that trace that had me face a given. A proposition that had come to the conclusion my vision was warning me, I had to lead and see it to believe it. It all come to be the only thing I could agree too was standing.

It was the message withstanding; I was hit back with a proposition. That is when I knew I hit a final revision, a dreadful mistake that became part of the mission. It was a dread long-lasting where everything that come my way was the last thing that had me facing an enlightenment.

It had me face another tread, a trend that reminded me there was no freedom no luck no passion just bad omen and open and shut case with a final declaration at the end of that manifestation. I was stuck in the middle of a troubled trace. It had me face another trip down memory lane.

Luck turned against me it had me dramatize every dread. For that thread had me forced to hit a dead end. It was part of a turn around that lined me up for a curse. It took me in and found me warning the corrupt I had no freedom nor foundation to win another resurrection.

The line was part of a presentation that handed me a vision. It created a dream that handed me a dead end at the end of that redemption. It served me a final revelation, no longer fighting back. I had way too many interests and projects back-to-back. I had no freedom to relive that nightmare.

After the trace became the end of the race, the journey was yearning it handed me a purpose that was uncanny. The foundation was to break the chain, for those who had no ending had no reason being. It was part of the drama that served me a willingness to hit me with an earnest approach.

For the corrupt knew all and I knew nothing. That is when I found myself hitting a warning. I was purely here to hit me with a warning and a forthcoming event that served me a yearning. It caused an effect and produced another final endeavour to that sacrament that took me in.

It faced me for a wrong move from within. Past that trace that handed me the incur, I was served me a challenge that broke the chain. leaving me no longer trapped in the middle of a siren. For that line up was part of a given reason; purely to hit the corrupt with a final momentum.

I was left to repeat an old case trace it at the end of that treat. I hit a threat that had me face a debt handing me the equation to fail every composition. The moment had me spared and the structure hade me overcome another outcome trapping me in the middle of a forthcoming riddle.

For the mission served me an evaluation to harm me at every destination. It gave me a chance to repeat repel force myself through hell. That is when I knew that every chance, I had the only thing that returned to hit me from within, was the last thing serving me when I forced my way in.

For what it was worth, and for what was to be given, the corrupt had no energy to hit back with synergy. They went too far, serving me wrong they took me in and repeated that sin. Assuming meeting me, will help them by attempting to use me to make it happen.

All it did was have them face me with a first and last choice. A chance for me to prove in advance I was innocent. I was targeted by an individual who worked for the system. A so-called saint who had vision and he needed to meet me to complete his mission.

Little did he know the game was part of a no show. It was a competition that ended in a proposition. It forced me to repeat redo and replace another trace at the end of the race. The only thing standing was the last thing that caused the effects. It had me withstanding a challenge.

It was a task, that had been left to the imagination. It became a part of an expense that was harming me at every destination. That very threat, became a siren to that silent treatment. It served me a yearning at every composition. A kind heart that cut me off, forcing me off the edge.

It had me fall straight into a final pledge, trapped in the middle of a storm facing another reality. Warning me the drama was drawn to me, because the corrupt saw me easy. It was about to unfold and the trace became a story that was to be untold discontinued; left to the imagination.

A journey that served me a difference had me rise above the indifference. A role, that confused the concept and had me reliving my destiny. Holding on to me for dear life, assuming that the method will cause an effect and bring the corrupt forward leading me towards a destination of destruction.

Where the trace became open to discussion. It was to bring forth an evaluation. But all it did was give me a chance to erase a final revelation. It had me waiting for the corrupt to waste another vision. It caused an effect and fed off me whole. Leaving me fighting a lost cause.

I was waiting for the trace, to declare a drama that was prewritten. All because the corrupt had a hidden agenda and I was victim to a sanctum that handed me remission to that admiration. For the corrupts final mission became part of a serious claim another game that had me remain silent.

I had to undo a claim with a review, continue on my path, holding to that everlasting cast. An entrance to second trial, to give me peace of mind. I fell into a trap that had me face the facts. I was being taught a valuable lesson. Never to look back or stare at that demon who saw me as a victim.

The trace handed me denial, leaving it to chance. A faith less likely for me to hit back. In the end of the final key was a clue it served a purpose. Forced me to hit back praise that hell raising trace. It had me on the edge, torn. No recollection or recognition not even a chance to return for admiration.

CHAPTER 9

◆ ◆ ◆

Awarding My Sovereign Soul

It was a challenge; I had to get through. Several were on my raider trying there hardest to frame me. Apparently, the lie will become the truth and the corrupt will getting away with hitting me and running. It led me astray; it had me face another harvest. A given gift with a challenge that paused.

It served me a well-deserved treat. It took me on a path that had me repent. It forced me off the edge repeating another trace, at the end of that force that caused an effect and forced me to hit back all while I repent. It gave me a chance to repent, representing a theme to that scheme.

It forced me off the edge straight in to a pledge, it was serving me an evaluation heaving at me at every informal investigation. It me forced to return and start fresh reaping a reward at every final encore. A request that caused an effect it caved in on the conquest.

It created a challenge that had me erase that case. It served me a willingness to embrace that ever-lasting informal trace. It was part of a given reason to hit back with an upcoming event. It served me well deserved energy that was harming me periodically. That is when I knew I hit a frail mind.

It presented me with a key, a trip down memory lane. A whirlwind travel that had me face a forthcoming spell. A space between the two handing me a one hell a chance to face my demons in advance. It was leading the pact and waiting for the trial to end and the trend to find its trap.

There was no gap in-between, just a challenge that had me face another trace. It had me create a new impact all so I can get back on track. For he who saw me as a threat and wanted to dig deeper, stalled for way to long I had no idea until I said my peace and had it unfolded and release.

It had me face a trace, tormenting me from within. All so he can win an inning, digging a deep hole, six feet under assuming killing me before my time will fix everything; but it did was open a porthole. It did not fix a thing; it made it worse. They got angrier and wanted to belt me with a curse.

They come out played then hid covering everything up again. Making me look like the perpetrator not the victim for every trace had a challenge and every given case had me face a replacement at the end of the race. Waiting for me to hit back because the assumption was part of a redemption.

In fact, it had me on the edge ready and willing to repeat and survive another feat. It was enough for me to override a trace and hand me a conviction to stand up and face an addiction. For every thorough response had me hit a given treason. Forcing me to return for chance to clear that trance.

For every trend had me hit a dead end, it was the one thing that served me well; from within. Handing me the key I needed to see was my way of accepting defeat and lean it towards a feat. I sensed I hit wonder a true reality. The plan, to harm me was in, it was to damage my spirit.

For every trace and every challenge had me foreclose that final draw. Where I get in and face another true rude awakening. A trace from within where eery thought took over that case and had me face another given there was always a troubled mind a lead to that trace had me erase

I was hunting for a key that served me well periodically. I had to find a way out of that mess and fight my way through only to witness I hit a final review. for my life was being tarnished by those who were varnished. Leading me to a destination that had me face another reservation.

All because the corrupt were monitoring me at every fight. They took me in, failed me from within. So, when I was about to create a piece and make it happen, they were on the other end leading the pact and starting again. Here I was back to where I was; ready, willing to make a difference.

From a very young age they would find ways to break my spirit. If it was not the kids bullying me it would be the adults facing me with the same trace that will leave haunted at the end of the race. I could not help thinking there was a demon trying to stop me from reaching my peak.

He kept entering my realm hitting one fellowship to the next. Lining me up for another death threat and hitting me wake up call. Waiting for me to fall fail so he can rise and reach up to the top hanging tight next to me biting my tail and tracking me down at every trial turning the tribe against me.

Every time he got me down, I was to face another haste. It caused an effect and took me on a journey that had me resurrect. What a waste, a given opportunity to serve the corrupt a scrutinized hold up. It had me face another first and last given; handing me a true rude awakening.

I was trying my best to hit the corrupt with a conquest. Waiting for the end to face me with a dead-end. Another trace to that case where the corrupt saw me as an easy target. I was hit with a trust fund, the family trust turned into a trough where it all turned to dust.

At Dusk until Dawn, I was stuck fighting a lost cause on my own. Waiting for the corrupt to throw me a bone. For me to lose my head so he can resurrect. I kept to myself left it to chance only to witness once again. I opened one hell of a door and created a piece. A challenge to face me at every feast.

They returned belted me to the ground, made sure I could not reach the top or make a sudden sound. So, when I hit the end the only chaos that restored my energy had me forced to feed off the trace. It had me face an imminent case. Last thing standing and the only thing that had me warned.

They created a piece in my head so I never catch up or force my way in. Leaving me unstable; losing my self-worth from within. I could not stand the fact everything was leading me towards the end of that inning. An evil thought that brought me peace had me face another feast

It got to the point they would claim the game. Hit with a crashlanding driving the corrupt insane. The cord was cut short; it left them stringing not only me along for so long. But the whole concept torn. The air became musky, smoke and dusty; debris where no one could see ahead.

I was no longer their daily bread. There was no key, or chaos nor even a chance to break me. It had me questioning every motive. I was silent suffering within, a given a chance to give in. So, when I reached my peak the only thing withstanding was the drama. A trace that had me forced to hit back.

It broke that chain, and the aroma ended up serving me a way out. It was strong enough to catch up and leave that pungent smell, handing me doubt. It was creating a challenge that had me reserved forcing me to repeat replace and follow up on another given trend in the end.

Where everything changed and I was left to repeat and rearrange. Handing me the evolution to return and break the corrupts constitution. It was forcing me to replace, repeat and face another feat. Facing me with a vision to revive and accomplish another goal so I can keep surviving.

All while I get back on track and reap a reward. It had me face another vision, while I track down those who hunted me down for another competition. Where I get in break the system and follow up on a vision feed off the competition break the silence and repeat after the fact.

The reaction created an abreaction, handing me an evolution to hit back. Where every restitution had me face another resolution. It eased my pain and stated a face a challenge that handed a brand-new impact. The game had changed; it challenged my perception and altered my perspective.

The alteration left me failing, it gave me a chance to create an intrusion. A presentation that had me forced to hit back with remorse. Where the corrupt no longer had the power to accommodate or even accumulate. For that distinction to that game served me a well had a desired impact.

It was leading me to a trace that had me face another intrusion to that manifestation. It caused an effect and handed me a journey that needed extra care and attention. Purely to keep it from losing its lustre, just to claim catch up and face a brand-new game. In the end I gave in entering anew.

A challenge that will eventually serve its purpose. I was left to begin a new service from within. For the best thing that ever come my way was the last thing that had me press replay. But no work went to waste, it had me face a trace. Giving me the permission to repeat and restore my energy.

I had to release that beast, and relive a competition. In comparison to the old the new and the upcoming clue. It had me on the trace if anything I was pushed off the edge of madness. Trying to get out of that doubt that took me down and forced me to hit the end of that trend.

It served me a difference, when I hit the end of that vengeance. It hit home run well beyond my years. The outcome was harsh the energy outlasted the old the new and the ongoing review. Forcing me to return repeat after the fact. It had me face a given a second chance to release.

That game that was forcing me to hit back, had me sustaining the truth. I was being hit with a curse I could reverse. It was part of a given to hand me the incantation, forcing me to hit back while I hit the end of that reservation. For that trace attached to my etheric chord was cut short.

Handing me a chance to repeat, repel and break that system; that put me through hell. The corrupt were on the move trying there hardest to hit me run. Leave me harvesting the wrong seed in the long run. Just so they can continue to breed more and leave me following up on an encore.

I wondered off, went for the drop, then rose above to claim a game. What I had to do to get through had me service the wrong clue. All while I gave in and faced another vision from within. It gave me a second chance to hit back in advance. Facing a trace on an ending that was pending.

For what was to come from that outcome had me dropping the bomb. They were reaching an analysis that had me remain strong. There was a challenge that had me face a trace; it caused an effect and presented me with a with trend that had me follow up on a dead end.

A follow up on another trend, became apparent. Where my journey led me towards a path that had me race to the finish line and hit back with the last laugh. For that trend served me well it had me hitting every forthcoming spell. Every key had me chasing a challenge a trial that will hand me denial.

For that key forced me to hit back with a final, united front. a challenge that will serve me well presenting with an ongoing spell. Pushed me in the corner and faced me with a trace that served me well at the end of the race. It caused an effect took me on a journey and presented me with a debt.

That given response was the beginning of a final vision. It handed me an invasion to serve me a trend it led me towards a journey that had me start again. I was pointing the finger at he who used me to get through. There was a challenge that shocked me it took me in and face me with a yearning.

A presentation that harmed me, served me wrong, it had me remain vigilant all while the rest remained strong. For what it was worth I thought it was the last resort it handed me a challenge to serve me a reality check at the end of that final bend. A proposal that had me face another trace.

in the end that trend became a vision that served me competition to face me with a review that forced me off the edge. It was handing me an enigma that trapped me in the end. All while I was in it to relive it, no longer on trial because the corrupt were on my raider torn at every viral.

They were waiting to see when they can return and face me with the same interrogation. For I was left to return face another given, feed off the trip and begin a new vision to the game. The trade was based on an accusation not on the truth and the assumption that became part of a redemption.

It handed me a revision to claim a competition. Because the one thing that had come together to gather enough information. Led me towards a journey that forced me to hit another interrogation. It was purely to push me off the edge, straight into a final pledge. Where my journey hit a keeper.

It had me embracing a case, forcing the corrupt to hit back, following up on a trade. I was to invite those who had me face a trace, trapped locked in; fighting another lost cause. Just to give me a key that served me well periodically. It had me forced to entrap, creating a journey that stirred the pot.

It had me lined up for a fake and false reading. It led me towards a path that caused an effect and praised me at every throne. As if hitting me again will land them a role leading me to a destination that will force me to praise and face another enigma at the end of the case.

Where this time around hitting me with kindness will give me the opportunity to release another beast and reverse that curse with a favour. Returning at every cause serving me well and presenting me with an upcoming spell. For a chance to return and belt me in advance was unravelling the truth.

Now that I am here and the trace was a given, it handed me a chance to hit back for no reason. It faced me for one whole new season, wrapping it up preparing for a round of applause. It was forcing me to return to break the system. It had me leave the corrupt suffering in treason.

Forcing me to write a wrong a passageway to the next pathway. I hit a road to recovery a challenge that had me face another trace. Only to witness the corrupt forced me to hit back facing me with a final raid. Leading me to a destination that had me hit a final renegade.

I was no longer ready to accept that ongoing debt. it had me fight back at the end of that trend. All because I was too busy wasting time trying to accept what was coming. There was a challenge that had me sense the only thing that served me well from within was the last thing standing.

For what I thought was part of a trace ended in terror. All because the corrupt saw me as their final vendetta. It gave me a second chance to reserve the right to hit back and face another trace at the end of the race. It was part of a pointless affair, that had me stand my ground.

I was facing another trace, a given reason to hit back with treason. For what was not meant to be had me facing another degree. I was taught a lesson, caught up in the middle of a trend that had me face a dead end, just to catch up. Meanwhile I make a difference and face the corrupt.

I had to struggle to catch up and save myself from a conspiracy. It had me facing another trap a written warning where corrupt happen because corrupt had already planned, I was the victim ready to fall into a trap that had me state a new fact.

It was part of my voyage that served me a cause, it gave me a chance to hit back in advance; praising the lord. My vision to return the favour and hit them with a composition. Created a combustion that led towards a mission handing me a proposition that served me well at the end of the mission.

Where the only thing standing was the corrupts final; a safe landing. They hit me with a challenge that gave me a relapse it handed me a force that served me a cause of action. Where in the end of that transaction there was a final abreaction before I hit that encore.

The plan to read my memoirs and use my words against me perse had become a hell of a gamble. The fact the words I used were not personal I saw the light I felt the pain I handed the corrupt another chance to push me in the corner and drive me insane.

I was warned of what was to come, I had to fight off a demon that was harming me in the long run. The challenge that was given gave me a second chance to hit back with a final treason. I was forced to follow up on another feast that had me release another beast at the end of that trend.

I had faith and the hope those who fed off me never had power to succeed, nor use me to breed. It had me stirring the pot creating a challenge that led me towards a journey that had me sweeten the deal. I was taught a lesson left to the imagination. A swipe to every forum with a foreign game.

It stated a fact, and put me back on track. The journey had brought clarity; it gave me a chance to hit back in advance. I had to break the cycle, take that final test before I hit an inquest. Where every evaluation had me face a mission where every thought will break every momentum.

So, when I hit a stage fright the corrupt no longer run for their life. For they found opportunity to fail me, it had me standing alone about to hit a final frontier. Where I get to see it, all come to be. Where the only thing that served me well from within was a witness who knew everything.

CHAPTER 10

◆ ◆ ◆

The Chariots On Fire

The lies, cheating, Gaslighting manipulation and the constant reminder I hit an Angry Demon. A challenge that kept me on the high striving to win every competition. In fact, I was not competing I made my mark I hit the end of my tither. Wanting to come back and repeat another wither.

Only to witness, I returning was huge mistake. The gas was lit the fire ignited and I was stuck hanging in there waiting for the corrupt to return and face me with the same old game. It was no coincidental event, what so ever. I was hit with a trace that left me informed of the case.

It was giving me the impression the corrupt had me on the edge. I was returning for a competition. The trace was a given the drama was a trend and the only thing standing in my way was the lead that had me face another bad day. It was giving me the impression the corrupt hit a final.

The drama took over and I was way too hard on myself; I was to give in and hand the corrupt a chance to finalize it all from within. They breached of contract broke the seal took me in and ripped me off. Where the deal was off the decision to leave me in dire straits was not open to discussion.

It gave them permission to repeat a competition. Where I hit a hold up and found myself locked in trying to get out of that death threat from within. I had to find a way to break that trace that hit a home run and faced me with a curse that served me well in the long run.

I was torn repeating a new term where my throne was no longer sawn. The long-term effect became a dead end and I had no freedom to retrace nor give in. Because the corrupt were too evil to hit back from within. They were feeding off the trend that had me face a dead end.

A decision to come after me and push me off the edge, was uncanny. It forced me to look within and find solitude from that trace that had me foreclose and force my way out of that morose. It gave me a chance to give in and hand me the impression I was hit with huge deception.

On the hope I lose my mind, for society likes to pick on

the blind sighted. The less people you know the weaker you are. You become a Target to those who find you interesting. Ready and willing to attain another seam to that scheme. Pushing you in the corner and serving you a theme.

For there is no Deity here, they treat you mean, to keep you keen. So, when they return, they march in attempt to match up and break your spirit from within. Dumping a whole lot of a drama in the long run. A trace that had me dumped, dumb me down make me weak.

Assuming that will bring them peace, an assumption had me face another redemption. Where I regret ever retaining that train of thought again. that had me face the last resort. A curse that served me well and presented me with a gift that literally put me through hell.

For those who sneak just to get a sneak peek, seek for peace. Assuming the presentation to that allegation will bring them peace. What a challenge I had to overcome, just to get in and regain consciousness in the long run. Where that claim had me facing a trace at the end of the case.

A train of thought that had me face a trial and an error. It caused an effect and faced me with trend that had me repeat a final vendetta. For when I reached my peak the earnest truth faced me and had me forced to return and press delete, at the end of the race.

It was invigorating to see it all unfold. Every challenge had me peak while the rest seek refuge. The trace became superior and the trend overcome another blend, to that bold entity that served me a well desired free ride in the end. A violation to the next common destination, in ways to harm me.

Where I was given the opportunity to release that beast at the end of my final days. It was indulging to see it all come to be, diluting that everlasting curse that had me reverse and face a trace that was trending. It was part of a true rude awakening, a trend that had me forever overcome a dilemma.

It warned me to give in and face another trace from within; every whim. Where the energy that served me well from within caused an effect and forced me to repeat, replace and face another trace at the end of that trend. It led me to release another demon that served me well.

I was never to state that fact nor even be pushed off track. I was taught a lesson by those who were competing with me. I had me suspicions assuming they had the power to undo and devour. I was left to repeat and challenge that trace that had me press delete.

I was denied access trapped in the middle of a tradition that served me a mission and claimed my presentation handing me key that served me well and forced me to get through without having to deal with the trauma the drama and the constant reminder I hit a final denominator.

That violation to hand me a constellation was giving the corrupt a dead end to that manifestation. A vision that unfolded before my eyes took me on a journey untold. Serving me a criterion that had me stand and deliver. So, when I reached my peak, the journey was unprecedented the trace released.

It had given me a test that led me astray. It caused an effect and brought me forward. Purely to resurrect handing me the okay when I reached the end of that given. A trace that served me well at the it was causing the right effects a division to a game that had me gamble every challenge away.

For the given mission served me a competition. It gave me peace and forced me to repeat a trend in the end of that final vendetta. Because it's the weak that make it to the end. That trend, become a dead end to those who want to see the weak break. All so they can get a chance to advance.

Where every thought pattern brought me forward, it faced me with a dream. A served well entity that warned I hit a final. Where every thought handed me the last resort. It was serving me a trial an error and a final vendetta. A certain degree of financial abundance to that everlasting encirclement.

For that entitlement had me face another finally. It was putting me in a position worse than the imagination. Creating an upfronted key the one I needed to repeat repel and redo. Before I hit an upcoming spell I was taught a lesson. It had me face a trace and pick where I left off.

I was living in between the lies the truth and the constant reminder the journey was uncanny. It had me face another trail, a redemption with denial; an exemption to the rule. A presentation to that violation that had me face a system that left me violated my mission.

It became universal and I found myself hitting a final request. Where I had to retreat and find my way out of that conquest. Just to catch up and face another conspiracy at the end of that warning that served me a yearning. Accusation was invalid the truce had me face another trace.

It was giving me the impression I was hit with an incantation, I was held hostage at every violation. A trace that led me to believe that every thought I was on was based on the journey that had me face a final. A long-term effect of bad toxic energy where it looked as if I was to blame.

In fact, it was a story plot, purely to push me off the edge and drive me insane. The story was a fable, my name not stable and those who had the freedom to embrace another trace made sure I never reach my pinnacle. Only to lose sight of the truth and face another dead-end fight.

My soul had me facing another test, it took me on a journey, that served me a wallow in the that willow. That is when I knew I hit a final review I was taken by surprise, and challenged by the demon in disguise. From an inner being that left me suffering in between.

It took me on a journey that stirred me and started a fight, that lined me for another key. A challenge that had me cornered ready to harm me. It ended in a follow up giving the corrupt a chance to hit me and run and leave me fighting another lost cause.

It was cut short; I was tested without a lesson in sight. The trace was based on a given that had me face another treason. It was hounding the corrupt at every season. That is when I knew they were not going to let me go unless they shot me with a heave and no show; so, I never see light.

Breaking my shine at every beam. Hit with a scam and a scheme in-between. I was not aware that it was played by the corrupt to hound me at every rough spot. For the journey was embraced by a case that was given it handed me a trend that led me on and pushed me off the bench.

Yet again I was stuck in the middle of a dead end. There was no fight it was a case that served the corrupt a chance to embrace. For those who knew could not wait to face me and enforce with another cause. For it had me cornered ready and willing to release another God willing feast.

I was pushed off the edge straight into a demonic pledge. It was based on a trace that led me towards a long-term effect giving me the impression I was torn in every direction. That trend was part of an intention that led me to an intervention handing the corrupt a chance to face a trace.

Where I was left fighting a loss cause, leading me to an early grave. Just to hand those who wanted a piece of the action a day to pleasure and a moment to remember.

Handing me an abreaction at every momentum. I could not help thinking I was being bribed by the possessed.

An unforeseen source, a spirit that remained to be seen. Dead or alive the seed was planted I could not define that trace, for what heaved had happened between the siege. A concept that took me in faced me with a traumatic effect from within. For all I knew I hit an ending that was trending.

A challenge that served me a trace, forced me off the edge. Trapping me in the middle so I lose my dignity, a follow up to the next vicinity. A reason not to live in serenity, but a given transition so I lose my intuition. I was forced to hit back with remorse so they can return and feed off me.

Leaving me living on the edge rough so I never pledge. It had me returning for another yearning reliving a nightmare so the corrupt can continue to count the waves. With every force there was a cause, I was stuck reliving a drama relying the corrupt to undo another review.

I was left to hit back with remorse, facing a cause. So, when I reached my pinnacle the only thing that had me withstanding. Was the last thing standing. It guarded me at every strength; it faced me at the end of that trend. Handing me a cause an effect so I can claim catch up and resurrect.

I was set up by the corrupt then given a reason to face a treason. For the drama was part of a rise, it gave me a second chance to restore my energy and feed off the trance. I was led on, left to remain strong by those who were rude, crude and ready to push me in the corner and break my spirit.

So, when I reached my peak, that energy that served me well presented me with an upcoming spell. I was left to hit back and face another imminent impact. So, when I caught up, I could undo another clue, create a piece and follow up on another feast. Handing me an indication there was preach.

My privacy was invaded my challenges were interrogated. The corrupt were instigating a thought pattern that served me a true raise; above and beyond. A willingness to stand free from that final degree. I was given a reason to hit back with treason. Catch up and follow up on another season.

For every journey took me on a path that had me face a true rude awakening. A trial from a daze that had me amazed, giving me the impression that the journey was uncanny. It handed me true rude awakening a given momentum that served me a return at every yearning.

For I was left to release delay and deny the corrupt access all the way. It had me face another trace; It served me an enigma to that stigma. Giving the corrupt a dead end to that scheme, that brought me shame in-between. In the end I took it in and accepted it all; just to define the odds.

Every method was considered as a win, and every challenge a warning from within. A trial and an error that served me well at every dilemma, delaying it all and facing me with a force to hit back with remorse. The journey that had me face a trace. Served me a willingness to hit back with sturdiness.

For that trial was based on the corrupts certainty, to that irony. A willingness to hit me with an entrance to unknown territory. It had me face an error, brought forward and forced me to hit back with a vendetta. A response to hit me with a time out, challenging me at every sprout.

Handing me the energy to get back up, get back on track and create a better impact. Nested in my head where the toxicity to that environment had me face another headspace. For I needed to replace the old start new and repeat that treat that stepped forward a and handed me the truth.

A trend in the end of that forthcoming event was unprecedented. For what I knew and what was true had no recollection to that final word. That description to that final resurrection had no revelation. Because it was covered up by the corrupts final destination.

Where the trace became a case, it was cursing my every being. Not only I had to remain silent but the game became quite interesting. There were several on my raider waiting for me to fail present me with a key so I can continue to sail. The trend had me face another given tradition.

For what was said and what was to come, it gave me a second chance to sweeten the deal and face another ordeal. For the corrupt were served well, handing me a replacement to that forthcoming spell. A case that gave in on the condition for me to repeat another competition.

I was to turn it around to my favour and win. Not allow the corrupt to ever enter my realm and hit me with the same entertaining game. I was hit with a clue; the trace became a tremor. The corrupt were belting me with a vendetta. It forced me to remain silent to a journey that handed me a siren.

A final chance to belt them in advance, had me forced to hit back with remorse. Served well faced me with an on-going feast. A challenge that had me forced to hit back with remorse, serving me a trace that led the corrupt towards a journey that had me forced to hit back with remorse.

For that trial and error created a final endeavour. A tradition that served me terror and faced me with a final vendetta. Another chance to belt me in the long run come to fruition, I was stuck hitting the corrupt at the end of that mission. It was part of the corrupts final repetition.

All so I can face another trace, a dying breed that needed to be replaced. It had me forced to hit back with remorse a challenge that had me reprieve, a given momentum that served me a sanctum feeding off the mission that led me towards a final competition. I had to face another reading.

A personal vendetta, had come to fruition. For those who had in for me were guarded by a huge conspiracy. That is when I knew I hit a final revelation, it gave me a chance to return and belt that creation breaking the tradition. Lock it in and find a way out of that mission.

Hitting the corrupt with a failed opposition. Was part of a warning, that had come to fruition, the past had returned for a repeat. Where the present had me face another restoration to that manifestation. Where the only thing that come my way was the last thing standing in my way.

Only to witness, I was part of a journey that had me face; another date to remember. It had come to my realization the only troubles that served me a validation was the drama that forced me to repeat a revelation. I was not able to remain stable, nor try my luck trying to overcome another rival.

I was to remain alarmed, stay alert no longer fret or feel the attack from that threat. For those who were on my raider, were warning others to stay on guard. Whenever they saw me create the piece, they will face me with a deception to break me at every reception; leaving me haunted by the past.

The way I was perceived was no longer part of that eve. It was a given, a present situation was undone and the only thing I could redo was the last thing standing right through. It handed the corrupt a chance to hit back in advance. Then prepare me for a hurdle, that had me immoral.

It had me on the edge wrapped up waiting to be saved. Not forgotten or forgiven, for every step was a given. Those who knew wanted to retrace, face me with a review. It gave me the opportunity to accept the fact the corrupt are two faced, are the true haters; stalkers trying to get back on track.

Where the only thing that had me face a breach, was preach. It was too hard to handle it on my own. I was fighting a lost cause, where there were several on my raider waiting for me to fail so they can sail through. For the corrupt had a chance to advance break the contract, and remain in a trance.

Leaving me forced to lock up, hide and pray for Genocide. A way of accepting defeat all the way. The kind heart I once had was over looked, there was no fear no faith the hope I once had turned into hate. I looked at the world, witnessed firsthand a prejudice society that will never withstand

That social endeavour had no room in my heart. For I met up with those who were on my raider stalking me at every trend. Waiting for me to fail so they can continue to pretend and sail. That trace served me a case handed me a clue, repeat repel and screw the corrupts method right through.

There was no clear path, my thoughts were overwritten and I was stuck in the middle of a failed system. The cleaner I was the more the corrupt returned to dirty me with an encore. It had me face another trace and return for one capacity to that enigma that served me well at every stigma.

The shame took over the game and the gamble hit me with a theme to that scheme. It was part of a redemption that served me the will to strengthen my soul at every trace that had me face and roam. Present me with a given where I was promoted and left to hit back for no reason.

The Networking I did was fake false and misleading. Noone was helping me succeed, for those who knew my intention were twisting my words around leaving distressed and destined to recreate another trace at the end of the race. They wanted me to end my life, with no repercussions.

With all seriousness I took it as a strengthening tool, I kept fighting for my life. Only to witness I hit a down fall and fell into a trace that led me towards a journey that served me well and forced me to look within and face the corrupt with a dead end and a death threat in the end.

They did everything in their power to break my spirit and devour. I was led astray, left broken wanting so hard to heal it so I can continue to prosper. I had nowhere to turn for that trace became a case that lined me up for an ending that was pending. A trace that had me face a new beginning.

For every step I took gave me a new positive outlook. Not worth leading, for whatever I did my gaols were ignored the game was misleading. I realized giving up and give in will give the corrupt another chance to get in and win another inning. The troubles erased and the drama took over the case.

I was stuck in the middle of a forthcoming event; it had me face a final endeavour to that debt. It was part of a prize-winning sector. I was to perish, break and left malnourished. Just to give the corrupt a chance to win a bet. Because I served well solved the issue they took it further.

I had to gather as much information, to give the corrupt a chance to confess. For it was the corrupt that was on my raider willing to harm me and leave me facing a path of no Harmony. I had to rely on the corrupts final investigation. Then take that as good faith; forced replace the case with peace.

When I was to catch up the only thing withstanding was the troubles that were hidden. So, when the corrupt served me well, placed me in a challenge that forced me through hell. I was to hit back with a trend that took its toll and handing me a time out to clear the old start fresh.

ABOUT THE AUTHOR

Panagiota Makaronis

I am not going to boast about myself, my education my family values or views. In the end what can I say life is what it is and everyone has their presentation.

What level of education I have is not important here, the fact that I have lived through death threats, dead ends, and the Demons in my head is enough for me to say! Good reddens, to hard labour.

Life to me has been nothing but expectations with several disappointments, on the hope I get somewhere trusting people when they were meant to help me was another story.

Having said that how many times have I heard people say I am helping you, I let my guard down and it ends up a never-ending Drama a story. Where if I was to repeat will end up worse than the first.

Every goal I set for myself so far though, I have achieved. This book is one of them.

But at what expense I had to endure, just so I do not lose faith in myself and in Humanity along the way. Others who knew could not wait to trace test my patience on the hope they erase my passion and end the race before me.

Because I was living and breathing in a society full of competitors, trying to compete with me and entering my realm on the hope they can harm me for they assumed that had more man power than me.

My theory is just to prove that the world is Governed, not just by everyone you meet but also by the way you witness and see yourself. It plays a huge part when you are about to end one journey and rehearse a new path.

A journey I wish not to return and replay, if anything I just want to move forward not look back and return for revenge. Because my opponent lost a fight and could not harm me so he decided to alarm everyone on the hope they cave in on it start an Allianz and harm me that way.

It left cursing the ones who were reversing and rehearsing, just so they can return stir the pot and leave me stagnant. Stuck in a world of my own sitting in self-pity, no way out unless I fought my way out.

That created more war in my peace because those who knew me, knew me well, fighting back was the only way they can prevent going through hell.

In the end all it did, was make things worse, for they were making mountains out of mole hills. However, the interpretation was enough for me to see I was on the right track the risks I took was based on not losing my faith or myself because others were doubting me and create anomaly.

They were haunted by me and my spirit they could not handle my presence or wait to see where they could hit me and run with a dead-end challenge. The only way out was to hold on to my dream repeat rebel and hit with an All might Spell.

I had come across several individuals who could not wait to break my fighting spirit, constantly on the move of how to kill me and my spirit.

The constant rejection, let down from those stalkers who had nothing better to do then follow me everywhere. Enter my realm just before I am about to make it happen, it got to the point I was failing every test because of it.

Eventually I gave in it was evident, let my Guard down on the hope and the condition there abuse and their method return and back fires.

Having to pick myself up after being pushed straight of the edge from so called Evil! Family friends and Associates, those who I call the corrupt.

What can I say a job is a job well done, level of education is based on life lessons? Everyone has a theory and so do I. Whether you agree is another story to just agree to disagree.

All the studying I did gave me an outlook, a method and outcome where sometimes I look back and wish I never entered but again I would not be here if I didn't.

The theory of here see and speak no evil to me is a lesson lived and lesson learnt. A challenge I can honestly say, it was testing a trace for me to embrace look back and erase. As I face my fears overcome another failure to that feast that handed me release.

As I look ahead and watch my journey unfold with a story untold, it will become a final phase to the next part of my truth. A challenge that will give me the indication I was on my path a feast to release peace.

Everyone is looking for answers and the hope to live through life with comfort passion and a reason without having to deal with treason.

My memoirs are based on my journey and life lessons, it is all in the book in the end only time will tell, what can I say will be me, keeping up with the programme my way.

Not the way they state it because I hesitate to wonder who is really saving me here. For in the end the matter of facts, is in my hands, because I am an individual. My thoughts are based on my life lessons and no one can challenge or change that.

I know every challenge has its presentation and what I see is I am about to shut one door and open another. Where my vision is no longer impaired and whatever is enlisted to get to this point is no longer in the back burner.

It belongs in my spirit it is mine I earned it! I am just messenger, just passing through the rest remains Ancient History added with a Mystery.

For those who read will understand read between the lines, because my point of view is a venture to next quest on hope I can make a difference to humanity for the next generation to read and interpret my vision as a composition not a competition!

Happy Reading!

BOOKS IN THIS SERIES

The Theatrical Melodia of my Life : Chronicle One

This book is based on my journey, the roller coaster I call life, my thought patterns, and my experiences. How I overcome so many turmoils, how I changed my perception, for it led me towards a destination that gave me tension. Where I felt I had no freedom or free will; all I had was failure. Added with faith, and the hope to overcome another fall. Feeding off the concept as I rise above it all!

B3stow™ Admonished; A Doctrine Of Defiance: Chronicle 28

The adventures continue, my journey up to now was a fight; with who? Only the corrupt knew. An assumption from within, made me see clearly, I was not wrong; my intuition did not serve me wrong. I felt my privacy was being invaded.

Devine Magnetism Awakening The Sovereign Soul: Chronicle 29

I was back on track stepping onto a new plane of awareness, after hitting a hold up, a knot I needed to break free from. The only way to do so was take a gamble. Only to arrive at a new state of being for the risk I took; has now paid off.

The Luminous Fire Of Discretion: Chronicle 30

A malicious cycle of events betrayed my trust. The scandal that put me on a journey that stirred everyone who was part of that contract. For those who assumed the road I chose was there's to consume, all by leading me on.

The Lioness Of Judah A Metaphor Of Strength, Misjudgment, & Truth: Chronicle 31

This is my metaphor the language of a burden, not reality."; it is my way of dealing with the pressure of what Civilization has to offer. My way, of letting Humanity know; what I perceive is what I believe.
"If I don't see it, I can't believe it, if I don't manage the stress then I won't be able to claim my truth."

Read Sample
Follow The Author

Panagiota Makaronis
Panagiota Makaronispanagiota Makaronis
Follow

Lifted By The Spirit Of The Mountain: Armageddon An Apocalyptic Revelation: Chronicle 32

A continuation of The Theatrical Melodia of My Life. Time to come to terms with the fact, it is the end of Civilization as we know it. I have lived through many pitfalls, the highs and low. I can't help thinking I'm a victim, a classic glutton for punishment. I keep going back for more not war, just to find peace.

www.ingramcontent.com/pod-product-compliance
Lightning Source LLC
LaVergne TN
LVHW012332100826
845148LV00017B/2120

* 9 7 8 1 7 6 4 4 5 8 1 6 0 *